Living with Schizophrenia

Dr Neel Burton qualified in medicine from King's College London, and has a degree in neuroscience from University College London. He is currently an Academic Tutor in Psychiatry at the University of Oxford. He is the author of two other books, including a textbook of psychiatry.

Dr Phil Davison trained at St Andrews and Edinburgh Universities, before completing his higher psychiatric training in Oxford. He has been a Consultant Psychiatrist and Honorary Senior Lecturer in Oxford for ten years.

Overcoming Common Problems Series

Selected titles

A full list of titles is available from Sheldon Press,
36 Causton Street, London SW1P 4ST and on our website at
www.sheldonpress.co.uk

Body Language
David Cohen

The Complete Carer's Guide
Bridget McCall

The Confidence Book
Gordon Lamont

Coping Successfully with Period Problems
Mary-Claire Mason

Coping with Age-related Memory Loss
Dr Tom Smith

Coping with Chemotherapy
Dr Terry Priestman

Coping with Compulsive Eating
Ruth Searle

Coping with Diverticulitis
Peter Cartwright

Coping with Family Stress
Dr Peter Cheevers

Coping with Hearing Loss
Christine Craggs-Hinton

Coping with Heartburn and Reflux
Dr Tom Smith

Coping with Macular Degeneration
Dr Patricia Gilbert

Coping with Radiotherapy
Dr Terry Priestman

Coping with Tinnitus
Christine Craggs-Hinton

The Depression Diet Book
Theresa Cheung

Depression: Healing Emotional Distress
Linda Hurcombe

Depressive Illness
Dr Tim Cantopher

The Fertility Handbook
Dr Philippa Kaye

Helping Children Cope with Anxiety
Jill Eckersley

How to Approach Death
Julia Tugendhat

How to be a Healthy Weight
Philippa Pigache

How to Get the Best from Your Doctor
Dr Tom Smith

How to Make Life Happen
Gladeana McMahon

How to Talk to Your Child
Penny Oates

The IBS Healing Plan
Theresa Cheung

Living with Autism
Fiona Marshall

Living with Eczema
Jill Eckersley

Living with Heart Failure
Susan Elliot-Wright

Living with Loss and Grief
Julia Tugendhat

Living with a Seriously Ill Child
Dr Jan Aldridge

The Multiple Sclerosis Diet Book
Tessa Buckley

Overcoming Emotional Abuse
Susan Elliot-Wright

Overcoming Hurt
Dr Windy Dryden

The PMS Handbook
Theresa Cheung

Simplify Your Life
Naomi Saunders

Stress-related Illness
Dr Tim Cantopher

The Thinking Person's Guide to Happiness
Ruth Searle

The Traveller's Good Health Guide
Dr Ted Lankester

Treat Your Own Knees
Jim Johnson

Treating Arthritis – The Drug-Free Way
Margaret Hills

Contents

Preface

In the middle of our life's walk
I found myself alone in a dark wood
Where my path was confused

Dante, *The Divine Comedy*

The aim of this book is to provide you and your relatives and friends with a source of information about schizophrenia that is accessible, clear and reliable. The journey through schizophrenia is often as lonely as it is difficult, but understanding and support can do much to make it shorter, safer and more bearable. By teaching you about schizophrenia, this book aims to alleviate any feelings of fear and isolation that you may have and to provide you with a realistic sense of hope and optimism. Simple and practical advice about day-to-day management enables you to take greater control over the illness, to make the most of the services that are available to you and – ultimately – to improve your chances of once again leading a healthy, productive and fulfilling life.

Dr Neel Burton
Dr Phil Davison

We would like to dedicate this book to our patients and to their carers, on whom they and we depend

Foreword

Unlike other medical illnesses such as heart disease, diabetes or depression, schizophrenia is much misunderstood by the general public. Selective reporting by the media of the rare headline tragedies involving (usually untreated) schizophrenia sufferers creates the impression that they are dangerous and unpredictable. This is untrue of the vast majority, who are at greater risk of harming themselves than of harming others, and merely adds to the heavy burden of stigma that they already carry. This stigma, principally born out of ignorance, makes the day-to-day struggle against schizophrenia all the more difficult, and it is no more justified than in any other medical illness.

Living with schizophrenia can be lonely, both for sufferers and their families. By learning about the symptoms and treatments of their illness, discussing it openly and seeking the help that is needed, they become better able to address their fears and regain personal control over their lives. This should in turn give them a better chance of leading a stable and fulfilling life and in many cases of making a sustained recovery.

Though information on schizophrenia is freely available in the public domain, much of it is hard to find, unreliable, inconsistent and – because of the uncontrolled nature of the internet – unnecessarily depressing. Much of what is easily accessible is aimed at scientists and health-care professionals rather than at schizophrenia sufferers and their carers, for whose benefit this book has been specially prepared. By leading them to a better understanding of the illness and its treatments, from medication to psychological and other therapies, and by guiding them through their day-to-day battles, it should serve as a giant first step on their journey to recovery.

Marjorie Wallace
Chief Executive, SANE

Acknowledgements

We are grateful for the support and encouragement of Fiona Marshall and Sally Green at Sheldon Press, our copy-editor Robert Whittle, Marjorie Wallace and David Gladstone at SANE, and Robert Dudley, our agent. The responsibility for the book's contents, and for any remaining errors and omissions, is all ours.

Neel Burton
Phil Davison

1

What's in a name? Schizophrenia through history

What does 'schizophrenia' mean? Do people with schizophrenia have two personalities?

The term 'schizophrenia' was coined in 1910 by the Swiss psychiatrist Paul Eugen Bleuler (see Fig. 1) and is derived from the Greek words 'schizo' (split) and 'phren' (mind). Although people often mistakenly think of 'schizophrenia' as a 'split personality', Bleuler had actually intended the term to refer to the dissociation or 'loosening' of thoughts and feelings that he had found to be a prominent feature of the illness.

Robert Louis Stevenson's fictional novel *The Strange Case of Dr Jekyll and Mr Hyde* did much to popularize the concept of a 'split personality', which is sometimes also referred to as 'multiple personality disorder'. Multiple personality disorder is a vanishingly rare condition that is totally unrelated to schizophrenia. Although schizophrenia sufferers may hear voices that they attribute to various people, or have strange beliefs that seem out of keeping with their usual selves, this is not at all the same as having a 'split personality'. Unlike Dr Jekyll, schizophrenia sufferers do not suddenly change into a different, unrecognizable person.

Although the term 'schizophrenia' has lead to much confusion about the nature of the illness, Bleuler had intended it to replace the older, even more misleading, term of 'dementia praecox' ('dementia of early life'). This term had been championed by the German psychiatrist Emil Kraepelin who mistakenly believed that the illness only occurred in young people and that it inevitably led to mental deterioration. Bleuler disagreed on

Figure 1   Paul Eugen Bleuler (1857–1940)

both counts and, in an attempt to clarify matters, changed the name of the illness from 'dementia praecox' to 'schizophrenia'. Bleuler believed that, contrary to leading to mental deterioration, schizophrenia led to a sharpening of the senses and to a heightened consciousness of memories and experiences.

It is as common as it is unfortunate to hear the term 'schizophrenic' being bandied about to mean 'changeable' or 'unpredictable'. Such use of the term must be discouraged because it perpetuates people's misunderstanding of the illness, and thereby contributes to the stigmatization of schizophrenia sufferers. Even used correctly, the term 'schizophrenic' does little more than label a person according to an illness, implicitly diminishing him or her to little more than that illness. For this reason, the term 'schizophrenic' has been dropped from this book and replaced by the term 'schizophrenia sufferer'.

Who 'discovered' schizophrenia?

Although Kraepelin had some mistaken beliefs about the nature of schizophrenia, he was the first person to isolate the illness from other forms of psychosis, and in particular from the 'affective psychoses' that occur in mood disorders such as depression and manic-depressive illness (bipolar affective disorder). His classification of mental disorders, the *Compendium der Psychiatrie*, is the forerunner of the two commonly used classifications of mental disorders, the International Classification of Diseases 10th revision (ICD-10) and the Diagnostic and Statistical Manual of Mental Disorders 4th revision (DSM-IV). Today these classifications are principally based on scientific research and expert opinion and, particularly in the case of ICD-10, on international consultation and consensus. As well as listing mental disorders, they provide clinical descriptions and diagnostic criteria that psychiatrists use to make a diagnosis of schizophrenia (see Chapter 4).

Kraepelin first isolated schizophrenia from other forms of psychosis in 1887, but this is not to say that schizophrenia had not existed long before Kraepelin's day. The oldest available description of an illness closely resembling schizophrenia is contained in the ancient Egyptian Ebers papyrus and dates back to 1550BC. And archaeological discoveries from the Stone Age have led to speculation that schizophrenia is as old as mankind itself.

How was schizophrenia perceived in ancient times?

In antiquity, people did not think of 'madness' (a term they used indiscriminately for all forms of psychosis) in terms of mental illness, but in terms of divine punishment or demonic possession. Evidence for this comes from the Old Testament and most notably from the First Book of Samuel, which relates how King Saul became 'mad' after neglecting his religious duties and angering God. The fact that David used to play on his harp to make Saul better suggests that, even in antiquity, people believed that psychotic illnesses could be successfully treated.

> But the Spirit of the Lord departed from Saul, and an evil spirit from the Lord troubled him.
>
> And it came to pass, when the evil spirit from God was upon Saul, that David took a harp, and played with his hand: so Saul was refreshed, and was well, and the evil spirit departed from him.
>
> 1 Samuel 16.14, 16.23

When did people first start thinking of schizophrenia as an illness?

In Greek mythology and the Homerian epics, madness is similarly thought of as a punishment from God – or the gods – and it is in actual fact not until the time of the Greek physician Hippocrates (460–377BC) that mental illness first became an object of scientific speculation. Hippocrates thought that mental illness resulted from an imbalance of four bodily humors and that it could be cured by rebalancing these humors with such treatments as special diets, purgatives and blood-lettings. To modern readers Hippocrates' ideas may seem far-fetched, perhaps even on the dangerous side of eccentric, but in the fourth century BC they represented a significant advance on the idea of mental illness as a punishment from God. The Greek philosopher Aristotle (384–322BC) and later the Roman physician Galen (129–216) expanded on Hippocrates' humoral theories, and both men played an important role in establishing them as Europe's dominant medical model.

> Only from the brain springs our pleasures, our feelings of happiness, laughter and jokes, our pain, our sorrows and tears ... This same organ makes us mad or confused, inspires us with fear and anxiety ...
>
> Hippocrates (460–370BC), in *The Holy Disease*

It is of particular interest to note that not all people in Ancient Greece invariably thought of 'madness' as a curse or an illness. In Plato's *Phaedrus*, the Greek philosopher Socrates (470–399BC) has this to say:

> Madness, provided it comes as the gift of heaven, is the channel by which we receive the greatest blessings ... the men of old who gave things their names saw no disgrace or reproach in madness; otherwise they would not have connected it with the name of the noblest of arts, the art of discerning the future, and called it the manic art ... So, according to the evidence provided by our ancestors, madness is a nobler thing than sober sense ... madness comes from God, whereas sober sense is merely human.

In Ancient Rome, the physician Asclepiades and the statesman and philosopher Cicero (106–43BC) rejected Hippocrates' humoral theories, asserting, for example, that melancholia (depression) resulted not from an excess of 'black bile' but from emotions such as rage, fear and grief. Unfortunately, in the first century AD the influence of Asclepiades and Cicero started to decline, and the Roman physician Celsus reinstated the idea of madness as a punishment from the gods, an idea to be later reinforced by the rise of Christianity and the collapse of the Roman Empire. In the Middle Ages religion became central to cure and, alongside the medieval asylums such as the Bethlehem in London, some monasteries transformed themselves into centres for the treatment of mental illness. This is not to say that the humoral theories of Hippocrates had been forgotten. Instead, they had been incorporated into the prevailing Christian beliefs, and the purgatives and blood-lettings continued alongside the prayers and confession.

How did beliefs change?

The burning of the so-called heretics – often people suffering from psychotic illnesses such as schizophrenia – began in the early Renaissance and reached its peak in the fourteenth and fifteenth centuries. First published in 1563, *De praestigiis dae-monum* (The deception of demons) argued that the madness of 'heretics' resulted not from divine punishment or demonic possession, but from natural causes. The Church forbade the book and accused its author, Johann Weyer, of being a sorcerer. From the fifteenth century, scientific breakthroughs such as those of the astronomer Galileo (1564–1642) and the anatomist Vesalius (1514–1584) began challenging the authority of the Church, and the centre of attention and study gradually shifted from God to man, and from the heavens to the Earth. Unfortunately this did not translate into better treatments and Hippocrates' humoral theories persisted up to and into the eighteenth century. Empirical thinkers such as John Locke (1632–1704) in England and Denis Diderot (1713–1784) in France challenged this status quo by arguing that reason and emotions are caused by sensations. Also in France, the physician Philippe Pinel (1745–1826) began regarding mental illness as the result of exposure to psychological and social stresses. A landmark in

Figure 2 In this 1876 painting by Tony Robert-Fleury, Pinel is seen freeing people with mental illness from the confinements of the old asylums. (Charcot Library, Salpêtrière Hospital Medical School, Paris.)

the history of psychiatry, Pinel's *Medico-Philosophical Treatise on Mental Alienation or Mania* called for a more humane approach to the treatment of mental illness.

This so-called 'moral treatment' included respect for the person, a trusting and confiding doctor–patient relationship, decreased stimuli, routine activity, and the abandonment of old-fashioned Hippocratic treatments. At about the same as Pinel in France, the Tukes (father and son) in England founded the York Retreat, the first institution 'for the humane care of the insane' in the British Isles.

How did beliefs change in the twentieth century?

The founder of psychoanalysis, the Viennese psychiatrist Sigmund Freud (1856–1939), influenced much of twentieth-century psychiatry. As a result of his influence, by the second half of the twentieth century the majority of psychiatrists in the USA (but not in the UK) falsely believed that schizophrenia resulted from unconscious conflicts originating in childhood.

Since then, the advent of antipsychotic medication, advanced brain imaging and molecular genetic studies has confirmed beyond any reasonable doubt that schizophrenia is a biological disease of the brain.

Yet it is also recognized that psychological and social stresses play an important role in triggering episodes of illness and that different approaches to treatment should be seen not as competing but as complementary. Thanks to this fundamental realization and the advent of antipsychotic medication, schizophrenia sufferers today stand a better chance than ever before of leading a healthy, productive and fulfilling life.

Treatments used before the advent of antipsychotic medication

Febrile illnesses such as malaria had been observed to temper psychotic symptoms, and in the early twentieth century fever therapy became a popular form of treatment for schizophrenia.

Psychiatrists tried to induce fevers in their patients, sometimes even by means of injections of sulphur or oil. Other popular but unsatisfactory treatments included sleep therapy, gas therapy, electroconvulsive or electroshock treatment, and prefrontal leukotomy – the removal of the part of the brain that processes emotions. Sadly, many such 'treatments' were aimed more at controlling disturbed behaviour than at curing illness or alleviating suffering. In some countries, such as Germany during the Nazi era, the belief that schizophrenia resulted from a 'hereditary defect' even led to atrocious acts of forced sterilization and genocide. The first antipsychotic drug, chlorpromazine, first became available in the 1950s (see Chapter 7), and opened up an era of hope and promise for schizophrenia sufferers and their carers. Since the advent of antipsychotic drugs, the use of electroconvulsive therapy in schizophrenia has become increasingly rare. Nevertheless, it is important to underline that modern electroconvulsive therapy is a safe treatment that can be highly effective in the treatment of psychiatric illnesses involving mood symptoms that are both severe and unresponsive to medication.

Where to now?

In 1919, Kraepelin stated that 'the causes of dementia praecox are at the present time still mapped in impenetrable darkness'. Since then, greater understanding of the causes of schizophrenia has opened up multiple avenues for the prevention and treatment of the illness, and there are today a broad range of pharmacological, psychological and social treatments that have been scientifically proven to be effective.

Schizophrenia sufferers now stand a better chance than at any other time in history of leading a normal life. And thanks to the fast pace of ongoing medical research, a good outcome is increasingly likely.

2

Who is affected by schizophrenia, and why?

Many schizophrenia sufferers and their families do not talk openly about schizophrenia, for fear of being misunderstood or stigmatized. This deplorable state of affairs can lead to the impression that schizophrenia is a rare illness.

In fact, schizophrenia is so common that most people will know of someone with the illness.

The chance of any given person developing schizophrenia in his or her lifetime is about 1 per cent or one in 100; and the chance of any given person suffering from schizophrenia at any one time is 0.4 per cent or one in 250.

Why is such a terrible illness so common?

Genes for potentially debilitating illnesses usually become less common over time: the fact that this hasn't happened for schizophrenia suggests that the responsible genes are being selected despite their potentially debilitating effects on a significant proportion of the population. The reason for this could be that the genes confer important adaptive advantages to our species, such as the abilities for language and creativity. Such abilities not only set us clearly apart from the other animals, but also make us highly adept at the game of survival.

Schizophrenia and creativity

Some highly creative people have suffered from schizophrenia, including Syd Barrett, the early driving force behind the rock band Pink Floyd; John Nash, the father of 'game theory'; and

Vaslav Nijinsky, the legendary choreographer and dancer. It must be stressed that such people tend to be at their most creative not during active phases of illness but before the onset of the illness and during later phases of remission. Similarly, many highly creative people have had close relatives who have been affected by schizophrenia, such as the physicist Albert Einstein (his son), the philosopher Bertrand Russell (also his son), and the novelist James Joyce (his daughter). Studies have suggested that this may not be simple coincidence, and that the relatives of schizophrenia sufferers benefit from above-average creative intelligence.

At what age does schizophrenia develop?

Schizophrenia can present at any age, but it is rare in childhood and early adolescence. Most cases are diagnosed in late adolescence or early adulthood. If symptoms indicative of schizophrenia occur for the first time in middle or old age, it is particularly important for the psychiatrist to exclude other conditions that can present like schizophrenia (see Table 5 in Chapter 4). This is not only because such conditions are more common in older people, but also because it is relatively uncommon for schizophrenia to develop so late.

Schizophrenia in men and women

Unlike many other mental illnesses such as depression and anxiety disorders, which tend to be more common in women, schizophrenia affects men and women in more or less equal numbers. However, the illness tends to present at a younger age in men, and also tends to affect men more severely. Why this should be so is at present unclear.

Cultures, climates and ethnic groups

Schizophrenia exists in all cultures, climates and ethnic groups, but its outcome is generally more favourable in developing countries than in developed countries. This is thought to be because tight-knit communities, such as those typically found in developing countries, are more tolerant of mental illness and better able to care for and support their mentally ill. This is important because it suggests that the attitudes of family and friends can make an important difference to the outcome of the illness.

Is schizophrenia more common in inner cities?

Schizophrenia tends to be more common in inner cities and urban areas than in rural areas. The reasons for this are unclear: it could be that the stress of urban life increases the risk of developing the illness (the so-called 'breeder hypothesis'), or that people with the illness have an overall tendency to migrate out of rural areas and into urban areas (the 'drift hypothesis').

Why does schizophrenia affect some people and not others?

There is no one gene that can be said to cause schizophrenia. Rather, there are several genes that are independent of one another and that, cumulatively, make a person more or less vulnerable to developing the illness. A person who is highly vulnerable to developing schizophrenia but who is never subjected to severe stress may never develop the illness. On the other hand, a person who is less vulnerable to developing the illness but who comes under severe stress may develop it. Examples of severe stress could include losing a friend or relative in an accident, being badly bullied at school or smoking cannabis (a form of physical, as opposed to emotional, stress).

The situation is analogous to that of many other important conditions such as heart disease or diabetes. Taking heart disease as an example, every person inherits a certain complement of genes that make him or her more or less vulnerable to devel-

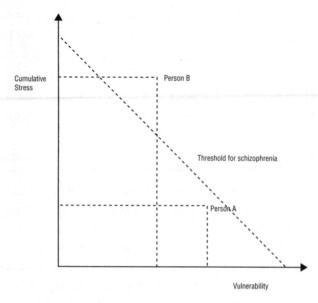

Figure 3 The stress–vulnerability model for schizophrenia. A person develops schizophrenia when the stress that he or she faces becomes greater than his or her ability to cope with it. Person A is highly vulnerable to developing schizophrenia but is only ever subjected to moderate stress and thus never develops the illness. Person B in contrast, though only moderately vulnerable, is subjected to stress so severe that it carries the person beyond his or her individual threshold for developing the illness.

oping the illness. Regardless of this vulnerability, if he or she maintains a healthy diet, takes regular exercise and drinks in moderation, then he or she is likely to remain healthy.

The role of the genes

If a person with an identical twin (that is, a twin who shares exactly the same genes) develops schizophrenia, the chance of the other identical twin also developing the illness is about 50 per cent or one in two. What this says is that genes do play an important role in the causation of schizophrenia, but that they are not the whole story. If genes were the whole story, then the chance of the identical twin also developing the illness would

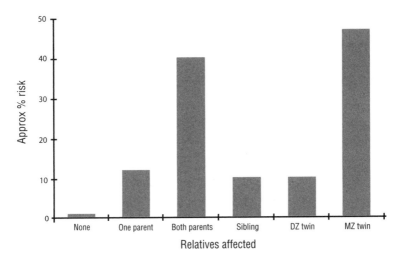

Figure 4 Lifetime risks of schizophrenia according to which relatives are affected. MZ twin, identical twin (a twin who shares exactly the same genes); DZ twin, non-identical twin (a twin who shares only half the same genes, like any other sibling).

be 100 per cent. The fact that the figure is in actual fact only 50 per cent tells us that, in the causation of schizophrenia, genes are quite literally only half of the story.

From Figure 4, it is apparent that a person's family history of schizophrenia is an important determinant of his or her vulnerability to (or risk of) developing the illness. If a person has no family history of schizophrenia, his or her lifetime risk of developing the illness is less than 1 per cent – a risk, as expected, broadly similar to that in the general population. If on the other hand a person has a parent or a sibling who has been affected by the illness, his or her lifetime risk of developing it rises to 12 per cent and 10 per cent respectively. These figures are only average figures, because many factors other than family history are involved in determining a person's lifetime risk of developing schizophrenia. Although not much can be done about one's family history, much can be done about these other, so-called 'environmental' factors.

The relationship between stress and schizophrenia

As dictated by the stress–vulnerability model (see Fig. 3), a person develops schizophrenia when the stress that he or she faces becomes greater than his or her ability to cope with it. This stress is often related to *life events*, that is, important events such as losing a loved one, going through a divorce, losing a job or falling ill. Though life events need not be negative, they are invariably perceived as being highly stressful. Thus, events such as getting married, having a baby or going on holiday can count as significant life events for certain people. The corollary of this is that life events are subjective: a life event for me is not necessarily a life event for you, and vice versa.

Life events      Schizophrenia

Figure 5   The relationship between life events and schizophrenia

From Figure 5 it can be seen that, on the one hand, life events can precipitate the symptoms of schizophrenia and that, on the other, schizophrenia – or its early or 'prodromal' phase (see Chapter 3) – can precipitate life events. For example, if a person in the prodromal phase is experiencing difficulty in concentrating, confusion and lack of energy, he or she is more likely to lose his or her job than the average person. Furthermore, the stress induced by losing the job may be great enough to tip him or her over into schizophrenia. So as you can see, the relationship between life events and schizophrenia is far from being a simple one.

Although life events can cause a lot of stress, most of the stress that a person experiences on a daily basis does not come from life events, but from seemingly smaller 'background' stressors such as tense relationships, painful memories (especially memories of physical or sexual abuse), isolation, discrimination, poor housing or unpaid bills. The cumulative effect of these stressors can be far greater than that of any single life event and may alone be sufficient to tip a person into schizophrenia.

A final point about stress, implicit in the stress–vulnerability model (see Fig. 3), is that different people are able to handle different amounts of stress. The amount of stress that a given person is able to handle is related to his or her genetic vulnerability to schizophrenia, but also to his or her thinking and coping styles and ability for social interaction.

People with positive coping and thinking styles and good social skills are better able to diffuse stressful situations – for example, by doing something about them, putting them in their correct context or simply talking about them and 'sharing the pain'. Again, the relationship between coping and thinking styles and vulnerability to schizophrenia is far from being a simple one, as people with a high vulnerability to schizophrenia are also more likely to have poorer coping and thinking styles.

What is 'expressed emotion'?

Expressed emotion can be thought of as a specific type of stress. It refers to the amount of critical, hostile or emotionally over-involved attitudes directed to the schizophrenia sufferer by his or her carers. Such attitudes often originate in a misunderstanding that the schizophrenia sufferer is actually in control of his or her illness and is 'choosing' to be ill. Alternatively, over-involvement can result from an unjustified sense of guilt about the schizophrenia sufferer's illness, and a desire on the part of the carer to 'share out' the burden of the illness. A number of studies have demonstrated that high expressed emotion is an important risk factor for relapse in schizophrenia, and that it can increase the risk of relapse by up to four times. High expressed emotion from carers may lead a schizophrenia sufferer to feel trapped, helpless or guilty, and the resulting stress may provoke a relapse of the illness. As with the relationship between life events and schizophrenia, the relationship between high expressed emotion and schizophrenia is far from being a simple one.

High expressed emotion ⟵————————————————————⟶ Schizophrenia

Figure 6 The relationship between high expressed emotion and schizophrenia

Figure 6 demonstrates that high expressed emotion can precipitate a relapse of schizophrenia, but also that it can reflect legitimate feelings of anxiety and distress induced by illness in a loved one. It cannot be stressed enough that parents should not blame themselves for their son or daughter's illness and that they should never lose sight of the fact that they are their child's most valuable source of structure and support, and his or her greatest hope for a permanent recovery.

Cannabis and other drugs

Many people with schizophrenia turn to alcohol or illicit drugs such as cannabis, amphetamines or cocaine to obtain relief from their symptoms and from their feelings of anxiety or depression. These drugs may temporarily blunt or mask symptoms, but in the long term they are likely to lead to more frequent and severe relapses of the illness. They may also delay getting help, including getting an all-important prescription for antipsychotic medication.

Research has found that **people who smoke cannabis are up to six times more likely to develop schizophrenia**, and that people with schizophrenia who smoke cannabis have more frequent and more severe relapses in the illness. This does not necessarily mean that cannabis causes schizophrenia, just as the fact that people who drink red wine are less likely to develop heart disease does not necessarily mean that red wine prevents heart disease (it could, for example, be that people who drink red wine also have healthier lifestyles). However, from what we know about how cannabis affects the brain, it seems highly likely that the drug can precipitate a first or subsequent episode of schizophrenia. For this reason, counselling about cannabis use can be an important part of a schizophrenia sufferer's care plan.

Other drugs that have been associated with schizophrenia include stimulant drugs such as amphetamines, ecstasy and cocaine.

Possible other factors

People born between the months of January and April have a 5–10 per cent increased chance of developing schizophrenia. This increased chance is referred to as the season-of-birth effect, and is thought to reflect the higher risk of viral infections during the winter season. This 'season-of-birth effect' is important because it provides some evidence that events taking place before or at the time of birth can exert an influence on a person's later vulnerability to developing schizophrenia.

Similarly, there is also some limited evidence to suggest that obstetric complications (complications during pregnancy and at the time of delivery) can increase the risk of the child later developing schizophrenia.

In conclusion

It appears that a given person's risk of developing schizophrenia depends primarily on his or her genetic makeup. However, this risk may not be actualized unless the person experiences a higher level of stress than he or she can cope with. This stress may be both a cause *and* a consequence of his or her illness. For example, a person in the prodromal phase may no longer be able to concentrate adequately and, as a result, may lose his or her job. The resulting stress may then push him or her beyond the threshold for developing the illness. Thus, the interplay of genetic and environmental factors in the causation of schizophrenia is far from being simple.

3

Symptoms

The symptoms of schizophrenia are many, and present in such a variety of combinations and severities that it is impossible to describe 'a typical case of schizophrenia'. In the short term, symptoms may wax and wane, with the schizophrenia sufferer experiencing both good days and bad days. In the long term, the emphasis may shift from one group of symptoms to another, presenting different challenges for the schizophrenia sufferer and his or her carers.

The symptoms of schizophrenia are usually divided into three groups: positive symptoms, cognitive symptoms and negative symptoms, as listed in Table 1.

Table 1   Symptoms of schizophrenia

Positive symptoms
Hallucinations
Delusions

Cognitive symptoms
Difficulties with attention, concentration and memory

Negative symptoms
Impaired attention
Restricted amount and/or range of thought and speech
Restricted range of emotions, or inappropriate emotions
Loss of drive and motivation
Social withdrawal

Each of these symptoms is fully explained in this chapter

Positive symptoms

The positive symptoms of schizophrenia consist of psychotic symptoms (hallucinations and delusions), which are usually as real to the schizophrenia sufferer as they are unreal to everybody else. Positive symptoms are usually considered to be the hallmark of schizophrenia, and they are often most prominent in the early stages of the illness. They can be brought on by stressful situations, such as falling physically ill, breaking off a relationship or leaving home to go to college.

Hallucinations

Psychiatrists define an hallucination as a 'sense perception that arises in the absence of a stimulus'. Hallucinations involve hearing, seeing, smelling, tasting or feeling things that are not

Figure 7   This is a self-portrait of a schizophrenia sufferer who appears to be hearing his own thoughts as if they are being spoken aloud. This is a special form of auditory hallucination referred to as 'thought echo' (SANE/Bryan Charnley)

actually there. The most common hallucinations in schizo-phrenia are auditory hallucinations – hallucinations of sounds and voices. Voices can either speak directly *to* the schizophrenia sufferer (second-person – 'you' – voices) or *about* the sufferer (third-person – 'he or she' – voices). Voices can be highly dis-tressing, especially if they involve threats or abuse, or if they are loud and incessant. (Carers might begin to experience some-thing of the distress of hearing voices by turning on both the radio and the television at the same time, both at full volume, and then trying to hold a normal conversation.) In some cases, though, voices such as the voices of old acquaintances, dead ancestors or 'guardian angels' can be a source of comfort and reassurance, rather than of distress.

Robert Bayley, a schizophrenia sufferer who has publicly discussed his illness, writes about his experience of auditory and visual hallucinations
As I open my eyes to greet a new day, voices commence with their attack – voices that discuss and ridicule my every move and thought, as though they can be heard from another room. They deride me, breaking down any feelings of positivity, gaining in momentum, reaching the very core of my mind. I also hear an officious, commanding voice that issues instructions, his vocalization resembling an automaton. Together they resonate and modulate, growing in their penetration, until they can be heard screaming. I also hear strange atonal sounds, and they in turn become akin to cacophony. As I rise from my slumber, the scenarios become more complex, as theatrical scenes are played out, and I hear all the individual characters reading out their lines from differing areas and locations inside the brain. Then these slowly dissipate, and I am left with the paranoid reality that is created by the automaton and the destroyers of Faith.

The next manifestation appears, as glistening beams descend from the ceiling, and the walls begin to close in. Objects inanimate are injected with life, and they gyrate and flex, as the floor ripples like the agitated flow of a river. I have spent hours transfixed by items of furni-ture that have conversed with me, as though possessing their own spirit, moving around without effort. Also, familiar people are translated into other forms, such as my wife into a painting or ornament. Demonic faces erupt from the ground, shattering in front of my petrified eyes. Existence becomes increasingly paranoid, as feelings of fear encompass, until the desire to mutilate can rear its ugly head, just to attain that sensation of release. Vast blocks of ominous tones hover over me, only to descend, as the ceilings come crashing down. I have spent so many hours existing within a world where actuality cannot easily be defined. I enter different dimensions, places where terror resides, a waking nightmare. As I endeavour to look outwards, my vision fragments into a thousand little pieces. I am left to put it all back together.

Delusions

Delusions are defined as being 'strongly held beliefs that are not amenable to logic or persuasion and that are out of keeping with their holder's background'. Although delusions are not necessarily false, the process by which they are arrived at is usually bizarre and illogical. In schizophrenia, the delusions are most often of being persecuted or controlled, although they can also follow a number of other themes. Common delusional themes and some examples of each are listed in Table 2.

Is a person with positive symptoms dangerous or unpredictable?

Positive symptoms correspond to the general public's idea of 'madness', and so people with prominent positive symptoms may evoke feelings of fear and anxiety in others. Such feelings are often reinforced by selective reporting by the media of the rare headline tragedies involving people with (usually untreated) mental illness. The reality is that the vast majority of schizophrenia sufferers are no more likely than the average person to pose a risk to others, but far more likely than the average person to pose a risk to themselves. For example, they may neglect their safety and personal care, or they may leave themselves open to being emotionally, physically or financially exploited by others.

How carers can manage positive symptoms

Positive symptoms can be particularly distressing, both to the schizophrenia sufferer and to his or her carers. Carers often find

Figure 8 This is a painting of the artist, Philippa King, experiencing an auditory hallucination of a voice that said 'Drop dead, drop-kick deadbeat punchline!'

themselves challenging the schizophrenia sufferer's hallucinations and delusions, partly out of a desire to relieve his or her suffering, and partly out of understandable feelings of fear and helplessness. Unfortunately this can be counterproductive, since it can alienate the schizophrenia sufferer from his or her carers at the very time that he or she needs them the most. Although this can be difficult, carers should try to remember that positive symptoms are as real to the schizophrenia sufferer as they are unreal to everybody else.

So, a more helpful course of action for carers is to recognize that the schizophrenia sufferer's delusions and hallucinations are real and important to him or her, while making it clear that they do not personally share in them. For example:

Person: The aliens are telling me that they are going to abduct
          me tonight.
Carer: That sounds terribly frightening.
Person: I've never felt so frightened in all my life.
Carer: I can understand that you feel frightened, although I
          myself cannot hear the aliens that you speak about.
Person: You mean, you can't hear them?
Carer: No, not at all. Have you tried ignoring them?
Person: If I listen to my iPod then they don't seem so loud, and
          I don't feel so frightened.
Carer: What about when we talk together, like now?
Person: That's very helpful too.

Cognitive symptoms

Cognitive symptoms involve difficulties with concentration and
memory that can cause difficulty understanding conversation,
difficulty registering and recalling information, and difficulty
thinking and expressing thoughts. Cognitive symptoms are
often detectable in the prodromal phase of schizophrenia before
the onset of positive symptoms and, though less tangible than
positive symptoms, can be just as distressing and disabling.
Compared with positive symptoms, cognitive symptoms are
less responsive to antipsychotic medication (see Chapter 7).

Negative symptoms

Whereas positive symptoms can be thought of as an excess or dis-
tortion of normal functions, negative symptoms can be thought
of as a diminution or loss of normal functions. Compared with
positive symptoms, negative symptoms tend to be more subtle
and less noticeable, but also more persistent. Indeed, they can
remain even through periods of remission, long after the positive symptoms have burnt out or faded into the background.
Negative symptoms can be difficult to pinpoint and, sadly, are
often misconstrued by the general public – and sometimes also

Table 2 Delusional themes in schizophrenia

Delusional theme	Explanation
Delusions of persecution	Delusions of being persecuted – for example, being spied upon by secret services or being poisoned by aliens
Delusions of control	Delusions that one's feelings, thoughts or actions are being controlled by an external force – for example, having one's thoughts 'stolen' by aliens and replaced by different thoughts
Delusions of reference	Delusions that objects, events or other persons have a particular and unusual significance relating to the self – for example, receiving a series of coded messages from the aliens while listening to a programme on Radio 4
Delusions of grandeur	Delusions of being invested with special status, a special purpose or special abilities – for example, being the most intelligent person on earth and having the responsibility of saving it from the effects of climate change. Delusions of grandeur are more common in manic psychosis (bipolar affective disorder) than in schizophrenia
Religious delusions	Delusions of having a special relationship with God or a supernatural force – for example, being the next messiah, or being persecuted by the devil
Delusions of guilt	Delusions of having committed a crime or having sinned greatly – for example, being personally responsible for a recent terrorist attack and therefore deserving severe punishment
Nihilistic delusions	Delusions that one no longer exists or is about to die or suffer a personal catastrophe. In some cases there may be a belief that other people or objects no longer exist or that the world is coming to an end. Nihilistic delusions are more common in depressive psychosis (a severe form of depression) than in schizophrenia
Somatic (hypochondriacal) delusions	Delusions of being physically ill or having deformed body parts
Delusions of jealousy	Delusions that one's spouse or partner has been unfaithful
Delusions of love	Delusions of being loved by someone who is inaccessible or with whom one has little contact
Delusions of misidentification	Delusions that familiar people have been replaced by identical-looking imposters (Capgras delusion), or that they are disguising as various strangers (Fregoli delusion)

by relatives and carers – as laziness or obstreperousness. For health-care professionals, negative symptoms can sometimes be difficult to differentiate from symptoms of depression, which are common in schizophrenia, or from certain of the side effects of antipsychotic medication (see Chapter 7).

As already discussed, schizophrenia can present in such a variety of combinations and severities that it is impossible to describe 'a typical case of schizophrenia'. In some cases negative symptoms can dominate the illness, but in others they may be

Table 3 Negative symptoms in schizophrenia

Negative symptom	Explanation
Restricted range of emotions or inappropriate emotions	Appearing flat and unresponsive to circumstances and events, or responding to them inappropriately
Loss of drive and motivation	Finding it difficult to do things such as cleaning, shopping, or participating in leisure activities. In more severe cases, being unable to fulfil basic needs such as bathing, grooming and feeding. Schizophrenia sufferers are sometimes accused of being 'lazy', but this is unfair as loss of drive and motivation can be symptoms of the illness
Social withdrawal	Finding it difficult to make friends or hold on to old friendships, resulting in a lack of intimate relationships
Poverty of thought and speech	Experiencing a marked reduction in the amount and complexity of thinking, and finding thinking to be difficult and tiring. Poverty of thought usually manifests itself as poverty of speech, involving restricted verbal interaction and a lack of spontaneous speech. For example, replies to questions may principally consist of stock phrases (such as, 'Oh dear, that's not good') and other short sentences
Impaired attention	Not being able to focus the attention for any length of time, thereby finding it difficult to take in information and complete tasks

altogether absent. During periods of remission, the severity of any residual negative symptoms is an important determinant of the schizophrenia sufferer's quality of life and ability to function. Negative symptoms are listed in Table 3. Compared with positive symptoms, they tend to be poorly responsive to antipsychotic medication (see Chapter 7).

How do the symptoms of schizophrenia progress?

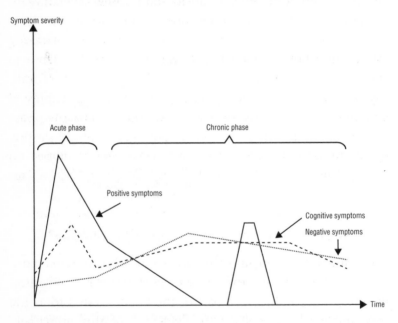

Figure 9 This diagram illustrates how the symptoms of schizophrenia may progress over time. As the course of the illness can vary, the diagram may not apply to individual cases.

The course of schizophrenia can vary considerably from one person to another, but it is often marked by a number of distinct phases (see Fig. 9). In the acute ('initial and short-lasting') phase, positive symptoms come to the fore, while any cognitive and negative symptoms that may already be present appear to sink into the background. The schizophrenia sufferer typically reaches a crisis point, at which time contact with mental health services is made. Antipsychotic medication is started and the acute phase resolves, even though residual positive symptoms may still remain in the background for some time. As the acute phase resolves, the cognitive and negative symptoms may appear to return to the fore and dominate the picture. This chronic (or 'long-lasting') phase, if it occurs, may last for a period of months or, in some cases, several years. In some cases it may be interrupted by relapses to the acute phase, particularly if the schizophrenia sufferer is not taking any antipsychotic medication. Common causes of relapse to the acute phase include reduction or discontinuation of antipsychotic medication, alcohol and drug misuse, high expressed emotion and life events. In some cases, the initial acute phase may be preceded by a so-called 'prodromal' phase, lasting for anything from days to years and consisting of subtle and non-specific abnormalities in thinking, feeling and acting (see Chapter 4).

What causes the symptoms of schizophrenia?

According to the 'dopamine hypothesis' of schizophrenia, positive symptoms result from an *increased* level of a chemical messenger, dopamine, in a part of the brain referred to as the mesolimbic tract (see Fig. 10). Evidence for this principally comes from two observations:

1 Drugs that increase the level of dopamine in the mesolimbic tract, such as amphetamines and cannabis, can exacerbate the positive symptoms of schizophrenia or induce a schizophrenia-like psychosis.

2 Antipsychotic medications that are effective in the treatment of the positive symptoms of schizophrenia block the effects of increased dopamine in the mesolimbic tract.

Negative symptoms on the other hand result from a *decreased* level of dopamine in another part of the brain referred to as the mesocortical tract (see Fig. 10). Again, evidence for this principally comes from two observations:

1 Drugs that increase the level of dopamine in the mesocortical tract can temporarily improve the negative symptoms of schizophrenia.
2 Older antipsychotic medications that can exacerbate the negative symptoms of schizophrenia block the effects of dopamine in the mesocortical tract.

The dopamine hypothesis has proved useful in understanding schizophrenia, but it says little about the actual cause of the changes in dopamine levels, and it cannot account for all the

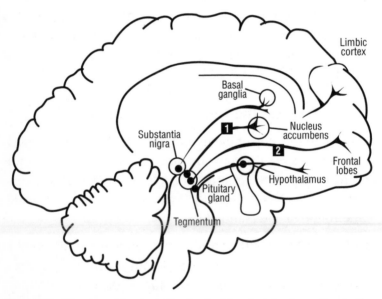

Figure 10 The dopamine hypothesis of schizophrenia. According to the dopamine hypothesis of schizophrenia, positive symptoms are thought to result from an increased level of dopamine in the mesolimbic tract (1), whereas negative symptoms are thought to result from a decreased level of dopamine in the mesocortical tract (2).

subtleties and complexities of the illness. Indeed, more recent research has found that a number of other chemical messengers in the brain, such as glutamate and serotonin, are also involved in schizophrenia, although their precise roles are as yet unclear.

4

Diagnosis

The majority of medical conditions are defined by their cause ('aetiology') or by the damage to the body that they result from ('pathology'), and for this reason are relatively easy to define and recognize. For example, malaria is caused by protozoan parasites of the genus *Plasmodium*, and cerebral infarction ('stroke') results from the obstruction of an artery in the brain. Unfortunately schizophrenia cannot as yet be defined by its aetiology or pathology, and so must be defined by its clinical manifestations or symptoms. As a result, a psychiatrist must base a diagnosis of schizophrenia solely on the symptoms manifested by his or her patient, without the help of either blood tests (as in malaria) or brain scans (as in stroke).

When should help be sought?

There is reliable scientific evidence that early detection and intervention in schizophrenia improves outcomes, and for this reason many local mental health-care services have an 'Early Intervention Service' specifically dedicated to this purpose.

The first symptoms of schizophrenia can occur at any age, but they most commonly occur in the late teenage years or in early adulthood. These symptoms are often preceded by an insidious so-called 'prodromal' phase, lasting from days to months and consisting of subtle and non-specific abnormalities in thinking, feeling and acting (Table 4).

Without the benefit of hindsight, the prodromal phase can be very difficult to recognize for what it is, especially as it so often occurs at an age when it can naturally be passed off as normal

Table 4 Prodromal symptoms of schizophrenia

Difficulty concentrating
Confusion
Decreased initiative and drive
Lack of energy
Flattened emotional response
Anxiety
Irritability
Depression
Sleeping late
Social isolation and withdrawal
Suspiciousness
Bizarre dress
Bizarre thoughts and thought patterns
Bizarre behaviour
Poor school performance
Poor self-care
Hearing voices

adolescent behaviour, relationship problems, depression or drug use. It is therefore important for parents, relatives and friends to 'trust their instincts' and to convince the person concerned to seek medical advice from a general practitioner (GP) sooner rather than later. Depending on the nature, pattern and severity of the symptoms, the GP may then decide to refer the person for a psychiatric opinion.

Valerie's story

Valerie is a 23-year-old anthropology student from Australia who shares a house with three other students on her course. Her housemates report that for the past six months Valerie has been behaving oddly, and that since the beginning of term four weeks ago she has not attended a single lecture. One month ago, she received a phone call informing her that her closest childhood friend, Chloe, had died in a motorbike accident. Since then, Valerie has been locking herself in her room for increasing amounts of time, banging on the furniture and apparently shouting to herself. Her housemates eventually persuaded her to see a general practitioner.

When Valerie arrived at the surgery, she was so agitated and distressed that she could not reply to most of the doctor's questions. The doctor was, however, able to make out that Valerie was hearing three or four male voices coming from outside her head: the voices were talking together about her, making fun of her, blaming her for her family's financial problems, and commenting on her thoughts and actions. According to Valerie, they were the voices of SAS paratroopers who had been engaged by her parents to destroy her. Valerie said that they were trying to achieve this by putting harmful thoughts, such as the thought of cutting her wrists, into her head.

Towards the end of the consultation, when the doctor stood up to hold the door open for her, Valerie screamed, 'I've seen your belt, they've sent you, they've sent you to distract me. I can't . . . I can't fight them any more!' and ran out of the room.

How is a diagnosis of schizophrenia made?

If a person is suspected of having malaria, a blood sample can be taken and examined under a microscope for malarial parasites. Similarly, if a person is suspected of having an abnormal rhythm of the heart, a heart tracing can be recorded so that the abnormal rhythm can be identified. On the other hand, if a person is suspected of having schizophrenia, there are no laboratory or physical tests that can confirm the diagnosis. Instead, the psychiatrist must base his or her diagnosis on the person's symptoms, which must meet certain agreed criteria listed in diagnostic manuals such as the International Classification of Diseases 10th revision (ICD-10) and the Diagnostic and Statistical Manual of Mental Disorders 4th revision (DSM-IV). These criteria are validated by scientific research and, particularly in the case of ICD-10, by international consultation and consensus:

- First, the person must usually have at least one clear symptom that is characteristic of schizophrenia, such as delusions or hallucinations of voices.
- Second, these symptoms must have been present for at least 1 month, and signs of disturbance must have been present for at least 6 months.

- Third, these symptoms must have an impact on the person's level of social or occupational functioning.
- Fourth, other psychiatric and medical conditions that can present like schizophrenia must be been excluded (see Table 5 for a list of such conditions).

How long does it take to make a diagnosis of schizophrenia?

The psychiatrist sets about excluding psychiatric and medical conditions that can present like schizophrenia (Table 5) by first obtaining a clear and detailed picture of the person's symptoms and his or her personal background, usually over a protracted period of time. During this time, he or she may also conduct a full physical examination, obtain blood and urine samples, and arrange for a brain scan such as a CT or MRI scan. In some cases, he or she may arrange for a second psychiatrist or other specialist (such as a neurologist or endocrinologist) to provide a second opinion. Only after the psychiatrist has confidently ruled out other psychiatric and medical conditions can a firm diagnosis of schizophrenia be made.

Indeed, after developing the first symptoms of schizophrenia, it can take several weeks before a confident diagnosis of schizophrenia can be made. This 'limbo period' can be one of the most difficult times for the person involved and his or her relatives.

If schizophrenia cannot be diagnosed in its prodromal phase, how is early intervention possible?

As schizophrenia is diagnosed from its positive, cognitive and negative symptoms, it cannot be diagnosed in its prodromal phase when these symptoms are still lacking or poorly formed. This, however, does not mean that the illness cannot be strongly suspected, and that appropriate treatment cannot be considered. Indeed, it must be strongly emphasized that early detection and intervention in schizophrenia can significantly improve the outcome of the illness.

Table 5 Conditions that can present like schizophrenia

Psychiatric conditions
Drug use – for example, cannabis, amphetamines, cocaine and LSD
Severe depression with psychotic symptoms
Bipolar affective disorder: severe depression with psychotic symptoms or mania (elevated mood) with psychotic symptoms
Schizoaffective disorder: more or less equally prominent symptoms of both schizophrenia and mood disorder (depression or mania)
Other psychotic disorders such as brief psychotic disorder, a condition which resembles schizophrenia but is relatively short-lived
Personality disorder

Medical conditions
Temporal lobe epilepsy
Head injury
Dementia
Stroke
Brain tumour
Infectious diseases affecting the brain
Endocrine disorders such as Cushing's syndrome
Metabolic disorders such as vitamin B12 deficiency

5

Coping with a diagnosis of schizophrenia

A diagnosis of schizophrenia is difficult to accept, both for the person diagnosed, and for his or her relatives. Like heart disease or diabetes, schizophrenia is a serious and potentially debilitating illness. But unlike heart disease or diabetes, or even other mental illnesses such as depression or panic attacks, schizophrenia is poorly understood and heavily stigmatized by the general public. This is in no small part due to sensationalist reporting in the media of violent acts committed by a very small number of schizophrenia sufferers. The reality is of course that schizophrenia is a common illness that can be effectively treated and that only rarely results in people becoming aggressive or dangerous.

Owing to the heavy stigma attached to a diagnosis of schizophrenia, some people may decide or be persuaded to consult a second or third psychiatrist – often at large expense – in the hope of having the diagnosis changed or reversed. Others may simply deny the diagnosis, and instead refer to their illness according to labels that they consider to be less stigmatizing, such as 'depression' or 'bipolar affective disorder'. Some people may prefer to tell others that they are in hospital because they have a brain tumour or because they are in a drug rehabilitation programme. Other people, particularly those suffering from prominent positive symptoms such as delusions or hallucinations, may altogether deny that they are ill. This may not only be because of the stigma attached to schizophrenia, but also because their delusions and hallucinations seem perfectly real to them, or because their symptoms prevent them from trusting or believing other people. For example, a person who is suffering from the delusion of being persecuted by the secret services may believe that his or her psychiatrist is a special agent in disguise and therefore that he or she is being lied to.

In contrast, some people experience a great sense of relief at being given a diagnosis of schizophrenia, because it enables them to get the help that they need, and to make the fastest and most complete recovery possible.

Unlike illnesses such as heart disease or diabetes, schizophrenia tends to strike in the prime of life, when people are likely to be full of plans and dreams for the future. In some cases, they may feel under intense pressure to succeed and be successful. As a result of being given a diagnosis of schizophrenia, people may feel that all their dreams have been shattered, and that they have betrayed those that they hold most near and dear. Mixed feelings of loss, hopelessness and guilt may give rise to a depressive illness and, in some cases, even to thoughts of self-harm or suicide. In such cases, it is important to remember that increasing numbers of schizophrenia sufferers do make a full recovery, and that many others are able to lead productive and fulfilling lives. Indeed, some schizophrenia sufferers, such as John Nash, the Nobel laureate in economics, and Tom Harrell, the jazz trumpeter, have even gone on to make unique and important contributions to society. You can make the future yours again, as you are doing by making the effort to read this book.

Robert Bayley writes about his experience of coping with schizophrenia
Despite the onslaught, there remains fertile ground. Areas where creativity can thrive. Physical discipline can also be applied, to aid the altering of the brain's chemistry. And beneath all this, the instrinic will to survive. To remain positive, when all around is coated with despair. For I believe that I can advance, I can develop strategies that will lead me into tomorrows. I will not be beaten. I will continue to create, make something beautiful from the extremes of madness. One day I will shout from the rooftops, all torment removed.

Finally, remember: you are not to blame for your illness, and you must not think that you have done anything to 'deserve' it. Do not let your parents blame themselves for your illness either. Just like anybody else, schizophrenia sufferers can have good parents, bad parents or absent parents. Far from being to blame, parents are often their child's most valuable source of structure and support, and their greatest hope for a permanent recovery. Schizophrenia is a common illness that is in large part genetically determined. It is not anybody's fault.

Many schizophenia sufferers find it difficult to accept that that they are mentally ill, and as a result they can be reluctant to help themselves or accept help from others. Schizophrenia is a serious illness and leaving it untreated can have grave consequences for your short-term and long-term mental and physical health. The fear, isolation, and difficulty in carrying out even the simplest of tasks can lead to a vicious cycle of neglect, depression, and alcohol and drug misuse. By accepting your psychiatrist's diagnosis, talking about it, reading about it and seeking the help that you need, you are taking personal control over your illness and giving yourself the best chances of a long-term recovery. Remember that you are not alone, and that many people have once faced a similar situation. Talking to these people can provide you with much-needed information and support, and help to alleviate any feelings of fear and isolation that you may have.

Although many people find it difficult to accept a diagnosis of schizophrenia, some welcome the diagnosis because it enables them to move on, get the help that they need, and make the fastest and most complete recovery possible.

Will I get better?

Although there is no miracle cure, schizophrenia can be successfully treated:

- About one out of four people recover completely within a 5-year period.
- About two out of four people get better but suffer from occasional relapses. The number and frequency of relapses depends a great deal on whether they continue to take anti-psychotic medication, and on the quality of the care and support that they are receiving.
- About one out of 10 people continue to suffer from symptoms on a permanent or almost permanent basis. Yet even in such cases, treatment and support can help to alleviate the symptoms and significantly improve personal functioning and quality of life.

Your individual chances of getting better are difficult to predict, but certain factors about the severity of your illness and your personal circumstances can act as 'positive prognostic factors' –

Table 6 Positive and negative prognostic factors in schizophrenia

Positive prognostic factors	Negative prognostic factors
Acute (rapid) onset	Insidious (gradual) onset
Onset at an older age	Onset at an earlier age
Clear precipitating factors such as life events	Absence of clear precipitating factors
Florid positive symptoms and associated mood disorder	Prominent negative symptoms
Female sex	Male sex
No family history	Strong family history
No alcohol or drug misuse	Frequent alcohol and drug misuse
Good occupational and social functioning before the start of the illness	Poor occupational and social functioning before the start of the illness
Good social support and stimulation	Poor social support and stimulation
Being married or in a partnership	Being single, separated or divorced
Receiving early treatment	Delaying treatment
Making a good response to treatment	Making a poor response to treatment
Remaining on antipsychotic medication	Stopping antipsychotic medication or not taking it regularly

factors that make a positive outcome more likely. Positive and negative prognostic factors in schizophrenia are listed in Table 6 – there are some prognostic factors, such as sex or family history, that cannot be changed, but there are also many, such as receiving early treatment and remaining on antipsychotic medication, that are within your personal control.

Life expectancy in schizophrenia is variable, and depends on the extent of the recovery made. Overall, the life expectancy of people with schizophrenia is reduced by about 8–10 years compared to other groups of people, but this gap is closing as a result of more effective treatments and higher standards of physical care. Cardiovascular diseases are the leading cause of death in schizophrenia sufferers, but they can be prevented through a healthy diet and regular exercise. One of the most important contributors to cardiovascular diseases in schizophrenia sufferers is smoking, so stopping smoking can do much to increase life expectancy (see Chapter 8). Other important causes of death in schizophrenia sufferers are accidents, drug overdoses and, in a small but significant minority, self-harm and suicide.

The suicide rate in schizophrenia sufferers is of the order of 5 per cent, although the rate of attempted suicide (unsuccessful suicide attempts) and self-harm is significantly higher. Factors that increase the likelihood of suicide include being male, being young, being unmarried, lacking social support, having high intelligence, having high ambitions or expectations, being early in the course of the illness, having good insight into the illness, and being recently discharged from a psychiatric hospital.

If relatives suspect that their loved one is suffering from symptoms of depression, then they should bring this to the attention of a member of the mental health-care team so that the symptoms can be addressed. Sometimes it can be difficult to differentiate the symptoms of depression from the negative symptoms of schizophrenia or from the side effects of antipsychotic medication. Nevertheless, depression is common in

Table 7 Symptoms of depression

Core features of depression
Sadness
Lack of interest and enjoyment
Feeling tired easily

Psychological features of depression
Poor concentration
Poor motivation and energy
Poor self-esteem and self-confidence
Feelings of guilt
Pessimistic outlook

Biological features of depression
Sleep disturbance – for example, waking up very early in the morning
Loss of appetite and/or weight loss
Loss of libido
Retardation (slowing down) of speech and movements

schizophrenia sufferers and it is best to have a high index of suspicion and to seek advice sooner rather than later. The symptoms of depression are listed in Table 7. See Chapter 8 for advice on beating depression.

What can depression feel like?

William Styron, the author of *Sophie's Choice* and other novels, wrote a book called *Darkness Visible* about his experience of being depressed. This is an extract from this book:

> In depression this faith in deliverance, in ultimate restoration, is absent. The pain is unrelenting, and what makes the condition intolerable is the foreknowledge that no remedy will come – not in a day, an hour, a month, or a minute. If there is mild relief, one knows that it is only temporary; more pain will follow. It is hopelessness even more than pain that crushes the soul. So the decision-making of daily life involves not, as in normal affairs, shifting from one annoying situation to another less annoying – or from discomfort to relative comfort, or from

Figure 11   'Blue iris' by schizophrenia sufferer Bryan Charnley. The petals are like three flags: one for hope, one for faith and one for courage (SANE/Bryan Charnley).

> boredom to activity – but moving from pain to pain. One does not abandon, even briefly, one's bed of nails, but is attached to it wherever one goes.

A minority of schizophrenia sufferers, especially those suffering from prominent negative symptoms, may in due course benefit from a period of rehabilitation to help them return to their highest possible level of functioning. Areas that need to be considered during rehabilitation include activities of daily living (e.g. personal hygiene, meal preparation, shopping), occupational activities, leisure activities and social skills. Sheltered employment programmes that use the place-and-train vocational model can significantly increase a schizophrenia sufferer's likelihood of gaining competitive employment.

Despite a period of rehabilitation, a small number of schizo-phrenia sufferers may be unable to live independently, and may therefore require supported accommodation. Such supported accommodation is often found in a sheltered home or a group home – a house shared by several schizophrenia sufferers and supported by a group homes organization.

6

Mental health-care services

The development of community care

Some 40 or 50 years ago, many if not most people with a first episode of schizophrenia would have been admitted to a psychiatric hospital for assessment and treatment, and some may have remained as in-patients for an indefinitely long period of time. In the 1950s and 1960s this so-called 'institutional model' of psychiatric care came under heavy criticism for isolating and institutionalizing schizophrenia sufferers, and thereby condoning their stigmatization by 'mainstream' society. This led to a trend of removing schizophrenia sufferers from psychiatric hospitals, in the hope of integrating them into the community. This trend, greatly facilitated by the advent of the first antipsychotic drugs in the 1950s and 1960s, continued throughout the 1970s and 1980s.

In the 1980s, such 'community care' came under heavy criticism after a series of headline-grabbing killings by schizophrenia sufferers. Although acts of violence by schizophrenia sufferers are rare, they tend to be sensationally reported in the press, leading to the false impression that this group of people are especially dangerous. The truth is very different: schizophrenia sufferers are sensitive and vulnerable, and in great need of care and understanding. A small minority may pose a risk, but this risk is far more often to themselves than to others.

Heavy criticism of community care in the 1980s prompted a government inquiry that culminated in the Community Care Act of 1990, a major piece of legislation that is at the origins of the present, more 'fail-safe' model of community care. According to this model, prior to discharge from a psychiatric hospital each person should have an agreed care plan and can, in a minority of cases, be placed on a community supervision order (referred to as a 'supervised discharge').

The advantages of community care are clear. By shifting the emphasis from a person's mental illness to his or her strengths and life aspirations, community care promotes independence and self-reliance, while discouraging isolation and institutionalization and reducing stigmatization. That having been said, a lack of mental health staff and resources can in some cases shift the burden of care on to informal carers, such as relatives and friends, and make it especially difficult to care for those most in need, such as the isolated or the homeless. The advantages and disadvantages of community care are listed in Table 8.

Table 8 Advantages and disadvantages of community care

Advantages	Disadvantages or problems
By focusing on strengths and life aspirations rather than on psychiatric problems, promotes independence and self-reliance	Lack of staff and resources can place a heavy burden on carers
Discourages isolation and institutionalization	Makes it difficult to provide care for those most in need, such as the homeless
Promotes prevention of relapse	Results in a shortage of hospital beds as scarce resources are diverted to community services
Reduces the stigma of mental illness	
Originally thought to be cheaper than in-patient care, but this notion has more recently been challenged	In some cases results in the mentally ill becoming homeless, or being housed in the prison service rather than in hospitals
	Poses a (possibly mainly perceived) threat to the safety of the person and of the community

One Flew Over the Cuckoo's Nest

Vintery, mintery, cutery, corn,
Apple seed and apple thorn;
Wire, briar, limber lock,
Three geese in a flock.
One flew east,
And one flew west,
And one flew over the cuckoo's nest.

Popular nursery rhyme

The film *One Flew Over the Cuckoo's Nest*, adapted from Ken Kesey's popular 1962 novel of the same name, was directed by Milos Forman and starred Jack Nicholson as the spirited R. P. McMurphy ('Mac') and Louise Fletcher as the chilly but softly spoken Nurse Ratched. When Mac arrives at the state mental hospital in Oregon, he challenges the stultifying routine and bureaucratic authoritarianism personified by Nurse Ratched, and pays the price by being drugged, electroshocked and, ultimately, lobotomized. Nominated for nine Academy Awards, the film is not only a (belated and contentious) criticism of the institutional model of psychiatric care, but also a metaphor of total institutions – that is, institutions that repress individuality to create a compliant society. It is such criticism of the institutional model of psychiatric care that, in the UK and other countries, led to the development of community care.

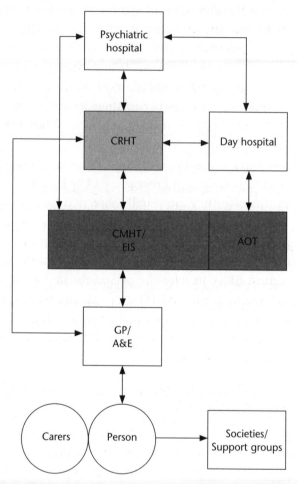

Figure 12   Example of organization of mental health-care services (local services may differ). Note that mental health-care services are organized to facilitate community care and avoid unnecessary hospital admissions. All terms used in this figure are explained in this chapter. CRHT, Crisis Resolution and Home Treatment Team; CMHT, Community Mental Health Team; EIS, Early Intervention Service; AOT or AORT, Assertive Outreach Team; GP, general practitioner (or family doctor); A & E, Accident and Emergency department.

General practice, and Accident and Emergency

If someone is suffering from symptoms similar to those seen in schizophrenia, the first port of call is usually the family doctor or general practitioner (GP). If the GP forms an opinion that a person might be suffering from schizophrenia or another psychotic illness, he or she is most likely to refer the person to specialist services – either to their local Community Mental Health Team (CMHT) or, in an emergency, to the Crisis Resolution and Home Treatment Team (CRHT).

A minority of people with symptoms of schizophrenia first present to Accident and Emergency (A & E) rather than to their GP. In this case they are usually screened by a casualty doctor, and then referred for assessment by a psychiatrist. Again, if the psychiatrist forms an opinion that someone might be suffering from schizophrenia or another psychotic illness, he or she is most likely to refer the person to their local Community Mental Health Team (CMHT) or, in an emergency, to the Crisis Resolution and Home Treatment Team (CRHT).

The organization of mental health-care services is shown graphically in Figure 12.

Community Mental Health Team, Early Intervention Service, and Assertive Outreach Team

The Community Mental Health Team (CMHT) is at the centre of mental health-care provision. It is a multidisciplinary team led by a consultant psychiatrist and operating from a team base close to the patients that it serves. Community psychiatric nurses (CPNs) and social workers are key members of the CMHT, often taking a lead in implementing and co-ordinating a person's care and treatment plan, and monitoring his or her progress in the community. Other important members of the CMHT include psychiatrists, clinical psychologists, occupational therapists, pharmacists and administrative staff (see Table 9). If a person is referred to a CMHT, he or she usually undergoes

Table 9   Key members of the Community Mental Health Team

Psychiatrist	The psychiatrist is a medical doctor who specializes in diagnosing and treating mental illnesses, such as schizophrenia, bipolar affective disorder, depressive disorders and anxiety disorders. The psychiatrist takes a leading role in diagnosing mental illness and formulating a treatment plan
Community psychiatric nurse (CPN)	The CPN is the member of the team that the schizophrenia sufferer is likely to come into contact with most often. The CPN usually visits him or her to monitor his or her progress and facilitate his or her treatment plan
Social worker	Sometimes a schizophrenia sufferer may be allocated a social worker as well as or instead of a CPN, in which case the social worker fulfils a role similar to that of the CPN. The social worker can also help to sort out housing and benefits and to ensure that the schizophrenia sufferer makes the most of any services and facilities that are available
Clinical psychologist	'Psychologist' is often confused with 'psychiatrist'. Whereas a psychiatrist is a medical doctor specializing in the diagnosis and treatment of mental illnesses, a psychologist has expertise of human experience and behaviour. A psychologist may spend time listening to and trying to understand the schizophrenia sufferer and his or her carers. A psychologist may also carry out talking therapies such as cognitive-behavioural therapy or family therapy, which are discussed in greater detail in Chapter 8
Occupational therapist	The role of the occupational therapist is to help the schizophrenia sufferer to maintain his or her skills as well as to develop new ones. This not only helps him or her to get back to work, but also keeps him or her engaged and motivated. Unfortunately, owing to limited resources, many schizophrenia sufferers are not allocated an occupational therapist
Pharmacist	Schizophrenia sufferers who also have a physical illness or who are pregnant or breast-feeding may find it particularly useful to speak to a pharmacist, who can help with information about medication
Administrative staff	Administrative staff are responsible for arranging appointments and serve as a crucial point of contact for both schizophrenia sufferers and their carers and other members of the team

Other forms of support that are available but that do not form part of the CMHT include support groups, telephone helplines (see Useful addresses) and the Citizens Advice Bureau.

an initial assessment by a psychiatrist, sometimes in the presence of another member of the team, such as a CPN or social worker. The skill mix of the multidisciplinary team means that the different parts of this person's life can be understood – and addressed – from a number of different angles.

Some people are reluctant to seek help and treatment, and as a consequence appear at the CMHT only in times of crisis. Paradoxically, these people often have the most complex mental health needs and social problems. For this reason, the responsibility for their care is sometimes transferred to the Assertive Outreach Team (AOT), a specialized multidisciplinary team dedicated to engaging them in treatment and supporting them in their daily activities.

Like the AOT, the Early Intervention Service (EIS) may also operate from the CMHT base. Its role is specifically to improve the short-term and long-term outcomes of schizophrenia and other psychotic illnesses through a three-pronged approach involving preventative measures, earlier detection of untreated cases, and intensive treatment and support at the beginning of the illness.

Crisis Resolution and Home Treatment Team

The Crisis Resolution and Home Treatment Team (CRHT), or 'crisis team' for short, is a 24-hours-a-day, 365-days-a-year multidisciplinary team that acts as a gatekeeper to a variety of psychiatric services, including admission to a psychiatric hospital. People with acute mental health problems are referred to the CRHT from a variety of places and agencies, most commonly GPs, A and E, and CMHTs. A member of the team (often a community psychiatric nurse) promptly assesses the person in conjunction with a psychiatrist to determine if a hospital admission can be avoided by providing short-term intensive home care. If so, the CRHT arranges for a member of the team to visit the person's home up to three times a day, gradually decreasing the frequency of visits as he or she gets better. Other than simply providing support, the CHRT can assist in implementing a care and treatment plan and in monitoring progress. If someone has already been admitted to hospital, the CRHT can also be involved in expediting and facilitating his or her discharge back into the community. The key features of the CRHT are summarized in Table 10.

Table 10   Key features of the Crisis Resolution and Home Treatment Team

Gatekeeper to psychiatric services, including admission to a psychiatric hospital
Prompt assessment of patients in a crisis
Intensive, community-based, round-the-clock support in the early stages of the crisis
Continued involvement until the crisis has resolved
Work to prevent similar crises from occurring again
Partnership with the schizophrenia sufferer and his or her relatives and carers

Psychiatric hospital and day hospital

Under the current model of community care, the vast majority of people with a first or subsequent episode of schizophrenia are treated in the community. If someone is admitted to hospital this is usually because care in the community is not an option. Possible reasons for admission to a psychiatric hospital are summarized in Table 11.

Table 11   Possible reasons for admission to a psychiatric hospital

Safety of the schizophrenia sufferer, his or her carers and the general public
Management of acute exacerbations (e.g. severe psychotic symptoms)
Management of physical complications (e.g. accidents)
Stabilization of medication
Establishment of a diagnosis
Alternative to community care if the schizophrenia sufferer lacks adequate support in the community
Respite for the carer

Of the small minority of people with schizophrenia who need to be admitted to a psychiatric hospital, the majority are admitted on a voluntary basis. This is either because they are happy to take the advice of their psychiatrist or carers or because they are frightened of their symptoms and have found the psychiatric hospital to be a place of safety (or both). In some cases, attendance at a day hospital during office hours only may provide people with a more tolerable alternative to hospital admission.

Figure 13 'Barmy days' by Paul Lake. Paul has experienced mental illness since the age of 15. Support from the SANE Arts Grant Scheme helped him to achieve his ambitions and he is now a successful artist. 'Barmy days' is a portrait of himself and some friends at the Brookwood Psychiatric Hospital. 'I wanted to show the positive side of the mental hospital and the way it allowed us the time and space to accept our illness.' 'Barmy days' has been exhibited at the National Portrait Gallery and is on permanent display at the Prince of Wales International Centre for SANE Research in Oxford.

A minority of people with schizophrenia who need to be admitted to a psychiatric hospital refuse to be admitted, usually because they lack insight into their mental illness. In many countries – and certainly in all industrialized countries – there are special legal provisions to protect such people from the consequences of their illness. In England and Wales, provisions for compulsory admission and treatment of mental illness are contained in the Mental Health Act 1983. The equivalent legislation in Scotland is the Mental Health (Care and Treatment) (Scotland) Act 2003, and in Northern Ireland it is the Mental Health (Northern Ireland) Order 1986. People admitted to hospital under one of these Acts do not lose all their rights to make decisions about their future. Soon after being admitted to hospital, the person has his or her rights explained by a member of staff, and can also ask for this information in writing.

The Mental Health Act 1983

In England and Wales, the Mental Health Act 1983 is the principal Act governing not only the compulsory admission to and detention of people in a psychiatric hospital, but also their treatment, discharge from hospital and aftercare. People suffering from a mental disorder as defined by the Act can be detained under the Act in the interests of their health or safety or in the interests of protecting other people from the consequences of their mental disorder. The Act defines mental disorder rather loosely as 'mental illness', 'arrested or incomplete development of mind', 'psychopathic disorder' or 'any other disorder or disability of mind'. To minimize the potential for its abuse, the Act specifically excludes as mental disorder promiscuity, other 'immoral' conduct, sexual deviancy and dependence on alcohol or drugs.

What is a 'Section 2'?

Two of the most common 'Sections' of the Mental Health Act that are used to admit people with schizophrenia to a psychiatric hospital are the so-called Sections 2 and 3. Section 2 is an admission for assessment and treatment and lasts for up to 28 days. An application for a Section 2 is usually made by an Approved Social Worker (ASW) with special training in mental health, and recommended by two doctors, one of whom must have special experience in the diagnosis and treatment of mental disorders. Under a Section 2, treatment can be given, but only if this treatment is aimed at treating the mental disorder or conditions directly resulting from the mental disorder (so, for example, treatment for an inflamed appendix cannot be given under the Act, although treatment for deliberate self-harm might). A Section 2 can be discharged at any time by the Responsible Medical Officer (RMO – usually the consultant psychiatrist in charge), by the hospital managers or by the nearest relative. Furthermore, the person under a Section 2 can appeal against the Section in its first 14 days, in which case his or her appeal is usually heard at a Mental Health Review Tribunal (MHRT). A MHRT is a visiting tribunal that comes to the hospital to hear appeals and consists of an independent doctor, a specially trained legally qualified chairperson and a lay person (a person representing the general public). The claimant is represented by a solicitor who helps him or her make a case in favour of discharge to the MHRT. The MHRT is by nature adversarial, and it falls upon members of the hospitalized person's mental health-care team to argue the case for continued detention. This can be quite trying for both the claimant and his or her care team, and can at times undermine the claimant's trust in his or her care team.

What is a 'Section 3'?

A person can be detained under a Section 3 after a conclusive period of assessment under a Section 2. Alternatively, he or she can be detained directly under a Section 3 if his or her diagnosis has already been established by the care team and it is not in reasonable doubt. Section 3 corresponds to an admission for treatment and lasts for up to 6 months. As for a Section 2, it is usually applied for by an ASW with special training in mental health and recommended by two doctors, one of whom must have special experience in the diagnosis and treatment of mental disorders. Treatment can only be given under a Section 3 if it is aimed at treating the mental disorder or conditions directly resulting from the mental disorder. After the first 3 months, any treatment requires either the consent of the person being treated or the recommendation of a second doctor. A Section 3 can be discharged at any time by the RMO (usually the consultant psychiatrist in charge), by the hospital managers or by the nearest relative. Furthermore, the person under a Section 3 can appeal against the section at any time, in which case his or her appeal is usually heard at an MHRT, as explained above. If need be, a Section 3 can be renewed for a further 6 months and then for a year at a time.

What is 'aftercare'?

If a person has been detained under Section 3 of the Mental Health Act, he or she is automatically placed under a section 117 at the time of his or her discharge from Section 3. Section 117 corresponds to 'aftercare' and places a duty on the local health authority and local social services authority to provide the person with a care package aimed at rehabilitation and relapse prevention. He or she has no obligation to accept aftercare. If he or she is judged to be at future risk of self-harm or harm to others, he or she could also be placed on a Supervised Discharge Order or Guardianship to ensure that he or she receives aftercare.

Table 12 Commonly used sections of the Mental Health Act

Section	Description	Duration	Treatment	Application or recommendation	Discharge or renewal
2	Admission for assessment	28 days	Can be given, but note that the MHA only authorizes treatment of the mental disorder itself or conditions directly resulting from the mental disorder	Application by ASW or nearest relative. Recommendation by two doctors (at least one must be Section 12-approved)	Person may appeal to MHRT in first 14 days. Can be discharged by RMO, hospital managers or nearest relative. Usually converted to Section 3 if longer period of detention is required
3	Admission for treatment	6 months	Can be given for first 3 months, then consent or second opinion is needed. Note that although treatment can be given, it can only be given for the person's mental disorder	Application by ASW or nearest relative. Recommendation by two doctors (at least one must be Section 12-approved). Importantly, the doctors must agree that treatment is likely to alleviate or prevent a deterioration in condition	Person may appeal to MHRT at any time. Can be discharged by RMO, hospital managers or nearest relative. Can be renewed for a further 6 months and then for 1 year at a time
4	Emergency admission for assessment (used in an emergency in lieu of a Section 2)	72 hours	Consent needed unless acting under common law	Application by ASW or nearest relative. Recommendation by any doctor	Person cannot appeal. Can be discharged by RMO only
5(2)	Doctor emergency holding order (person already admitted to hospital on an informal basis)	72 hours	Consent needed unless acting under common law	Recommendation by the RMO or his or her nominated deputy	Person cannot appeal. Can be discharged by RMO only
5(4)	Nurse emergency holding order (person already being informally treated for a mental disorder)	6 hours	Consent needed unless acting under common law	Recommendation from a registered mental nurse	Person cannot appeal
117	Automatically applies if someone has been detained under Section 3. Under Section 117 it is the duty of the local health authority and the local social services authority to provide after-care. Unlike under supervised discharge, there is no obligation for the person to accept it. Supervised discharge can apply only to a person having been detained under a treatment section				

MHA, Mental Health Act; ASW, Approved Social Worker; Section 12-approved, Section 12 approval is usually granted to psychiatrists having obtained Membership of the Royal College of Psychiatrists (MRCPsych) or having more than 3 years experience; RMO, Responsible Medical Officer, usually the consultant in charge; MHRT, Mental Health Review Tribunal, consisting of an independent doctor, a legal person and a lay person.

What other sections of the Mental Health Act are commonly used?

Commonly used sections of the Mental Health Act are summarized in Table 12.

Reform of the Mental Health Act

In July 1998, the government announced its intention to reform the Mental Health Act 1983, and produced a revised draft bill in September 2004. Important proposals included plans to:

- Broaden the range of people liable to compulsory hospital detention and treatment to include those judged to be at high risk to themselves or to others, e.g. people with antisocial personality disorder.
- Extend compulsory treatment to the community.
- Introduce additional safeguards, e.g. an extended role for independent tribunals to look at care plans for all those detained over 28 days.

Many mental health charities and mental health professionals felt that the reform was driven more by concern for public safety than by an interest in the care of people with mental illnesses. In particular they felt that, by confounding health care and crime prevention, the draft bill could put civil liberties at risk and persecute and stigmatize those most in need of care. For this and other reasons, the government announced in 2006 that it had shelved plans to reform the Mental Health Act and that it intended instead to introduce a shortened and streamlined bill to amend it.

The Care Programme Approach

The longer-term care and treatment of people accepted into specialist mental health-care services is usually planned at one or several Care Programme Approach (CPA) meetings attended by both the schizophrenia sufferer and his or her carers. These

meetings are useful to establish the context of the schizophrenia sufferer's illness, evaluate his or her current personal
circumstances, assess his or her medical, psychological and
social needs, and formulate a detailed care and treatment plan
to ensure that these needs are met. As well as ensuring that
the schizophrenia sufferer takes his or her medication and is
regularly seen by a psychiatrist or CPN, this care and treatment
plan may involve a number of psychological or social interventions such as attendance at self-help groups, carer education
and support, home help, cognitive-behavioural therapy and
rehabilitation. A care co-ordinator, most often a CPN or social
worker, is appointed to ensure that the care and treatment plan
is implemented and revised in light of changing needs and circumstances. The people who generally attend CPA meetings are
listed in Table 13.

At the outcome of a CPA meeting the schizophrenia sufferer
should feel that his or her needs and circumstances have been
understood, and that the care plan that he or she has helped to
formulate closely reflects these.

Table 13 People who regularly attend Care Programme Approach meetings

The schizophrenia sufferer
Relatives or advocates of the schizophrenia sufferer
The Responsible Medical Officer (usually a consultant psychiatrist)
Other psychiatrists
The GP
The care co-ordinator (most often a community psychiatric nurse or social worker)
A community psychiatric nurse
A social worker
An occupational therapist
A worker from the schizophrenia sufferer's residential home, day placement or home

7

Antipsychotic medication

Although there is no miracle cure for schizophrenia, the illness can be treated, and three out of four schizophrenia sufferers can expect either to recover completely or to improve significantly. Antipsychotic medication is the mainstay of treatment, but psychosocial treatments such as patient and family education, self-help groups, illness self-management, social and vocational skills training, and cognitive-behavioural therapy can also play an important role in reducing symptoms, preventing relapse and re-hospitalization, and helping you to take control over your illness and – ultimately – rebuild your life. Psychosocial treatments are discussed in Chapter 8.

Antipsychotic medication

How antipsychotic medication works

You may recall from Chapter 3 that, according to the dopamine hypothesis, the positive symptoms of schizophrenia result from an increased level of the chemical messenger dopamine in a part of the brain called the mesolimbic tract. Antipsychotics are effective in the treatment of positive symptoms principally because they block the effects of dopamine in the mesolimbic tract.

How effective is antipsychotic medication?

Antipsychotic medication is effective in controlling positive symptoms in about 70–80 per cent of schizophrenia sufferers, although it often takes several days before any effects are evident. Until then the schizophrenia sufferer may benefit from taking a sedative such as lorazepam if he or she is distressed or agitated. In some cases, several antipsychotics may need to be tried before the one that is best for them can be found, and this involves an inevitable period of 'trial and error'. Unfortunately, antipsychotic medication has relatively little effect on the cognitive and, especially, the negative symptoms of schizophrenia.

Is antipsychotic medication always needed?

Although non-pharmacological, psychosocial treatments have an important role to play in the management of schizophrenia (see Chapter 8), antipsychotic medication is always needed. Indeed, scientific research has conclusively demonstrated that long-term antipsychotic treatment reduces rates of relapse and re-hospitalization in a substantial number of schizophrenia sufferers.

Many people understandably do not like taking too much medication, because they are frightened of becoming addicted to pills, or frightened of suffering undesirable side effects. Like all medication, antipsychotic medication can have side effects, but it is not in any sense addictive. Adequate management of the situation involves balancing the risks and benefits of treatment with antipsychotic medication and reassessing that balance in light of changing circumstances. It is important to remember that not all people taking antipsychotic medication suffer from side effects, and that for many of those who do, the side effects are only mild or temporary.

Which antipsychotic medication?

Current treatment guidelines for the treatment of schizophrenia recommend starting on one of the more recent (so-called 'atypical') antipsychotics, which, compared with the older (so-called 'typical') antipsychotics, are less likely to produce certain types of disturbing side effects called extrapyramidal side effects (see below). The more recent atypical antipsychotics may have greater efficacy against cognitive and negative symptoms than the older typical antipsychotics. That having been said, many schizophrenia sufferers who have been on antipsychotic medication for many years choose to remain on the older typical antipsychotics because they find them to be both effective and tolerable.

There are several atypical antipsychotics, and risperidone, olanzapine and quetiapine are the most commonly prescribed ones. While these antipsychotics are on balance similarly effective, each has a slightly different side-effect profile, which the schizophrenia sufferer, aided by his or her doctor, can choose from. In addition, some antipsychotics come in different forms that can make taking them easier. For example, they may come in liquid form or as an oral dispersable tablet (ODT) that dissolves in the mouth. The various factors involved in choosing an antipsychotic medication are listed in Table 14.

As previously mentioned, some people may need to try several antipsychotics before finding the one that is best for them, and this involves an inevitable period of 'trial and error'. This can be a particularly difficult time because different antipsychotics

Table 14: Principal factors involved in choosing an antipsychotic

Initially
Particular side effect(s) that the schizophrenia sufferer is keen to avoid
Any previous side effects that he or she found to be unacceptable
Difficulties that he or she anticipates in taking the antipsychotic in standard tablet form

Later in the course of treatment
Effectiveness of antipsychotic in controlling the schizophrenia sufferer's symptoms
Current side effects that he or she finds to be unacceptable
Difficulties that he or she has in taking the antipsychotic in standard tablet form

may need to be taken at different times and may have different effects and different side effects. Although sharing experiences can be useful, it is important not to be overly influenced by other people's individual experiences with antipsychotic medication. Every person is unique, and for this reason there is no one antipsychotic that best suits all.

Questions to ask your doctor before you start on an antipsychotic

Questions that you might want to ask your doctor before you start taking an antipsychotic medication include:

- How will it help me?
- How do I take it?
- How long will it take to work?
- What side effects do I risk, and can I do anything to avoid or reduce them?
- Whom should I talk to if there is a problem?
- How long do I need to take it for?

Side effects of antipsychotic medication

As previously mentioned, antipsychotics are effective in the treatment of positive symptoms such as hallucinations and delusions principally because they block the effects of dopamine in the mesolimbic tract. Unfortunately, they can block the effects of dopamine in other brain tracts too, and this can lead to a number of side effects.

- If an antipsychotic blocks the effects of dopamine in the nigrostriatal tract (see Fig. 14), this can lead to extrapyramidal side effects which involve a disturbance of voluntary muscle function. The four recognized types of extrapyramidal side effects are summarized in Table 15.
- If an antipsychotic blocks the effects of dopamine in the tuberoinfundibular tract, this can lead to an increase in

the hormone prolactin (hyperprolactinaemia), which might cause loss of libido and, in men, erectile dysfunction.

- Finally, if an antipsychotic blocks the effects of dopamine in the mesocortical tract, this can exacerbate the negative symptoms of schizophrenia, which are caused by a decrease in dopamine in this tract (see Chapter 3).

Antipsychotics can also interfere with other neurotransmitters in the brain, and this may potentially result in further side effects. An important and common side effect is sedation, although some degree of sedation can be beneficial in people with distressing positive symptoms. Another important and common side effect is weight gain, which can place people at long-term risk of heart disease and diabetes. For these reasons,

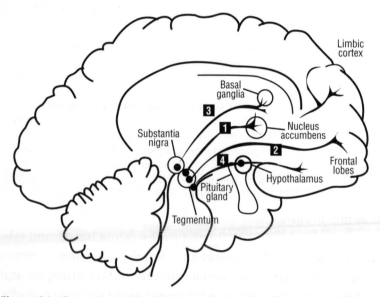

Figure 14 Dopamine projections in the brain, showing the mesolimbic tract (1) (positive symptoms of schizophrenia), the mesocortical tract (2) (negative symptoms of schizophrenia), the nigrostriatal tract (3) (extrapyramidal side effects of antipsychotic medication) and the tuberoinfundibular tract (4) (sexual side effects of antipsychotic medication).

Table 15: Extrapyramidal side effects of antipsychotics

Acute dystonias	Acute dystonias involve painful contractions of a muscle or muscle group, most commonly in the neck, eyes and trunk. They are usually easily recognized and successfully treated with anticholinergic medication such as procyclidine, orphenadrine or benzhexol
Akathisia	Akathisia involves a distressing feeling of inner restlessness, manifested by fidgety leg movements, shuffling of the feet and pacing. As akathisia is readily confused with the positive symptoms of schizophrenia, it can sometimes be difficult to recognize. Treatment usually involves reducing the dose of antipsychotic or changing to another antipsychotic
Parkinson-like symptoms	Parkinson-like symptoms principally involve three features: tremor, muscular rigidity and difficulty starting movements. Parkinson-like symptoms may respond to anticholinergic medication, although it is often preferable to reduce the dose of antipsychotic or change to another antipsychotic
Tardive dyskinesia	Tardive dyskinesia usually occurs after several months or years of antipsychotic treatment and is often irreversible. It involves involuntary, repetitive, purposeless movements of the tongue, lips, face, trunk and extremities. The movements may be generalized or affect only certain muscle groups, typically the muscles around the mouth. There is no consistently beneficial treatment, and the condition may be exacerbated by anticholinergic medication. Since the advent of atypical antipsychotics, tardive dyskinesia has become considerably less common

it is important to have your physical health monitored, avoid smoking, develop and maintain healthy eating habits, and take regular exercise. Other common side effects of antipsychotics include orthostatic hypotension (dizziness upon sitting up and standing) and so-called anticholinergic side effects such as dry mouth, blurred vision and constipation.

Any side effects that have not been mentioned are comparatively uncommon and may vary from one antipsychotic to another.

Table 16 Comparison of the side-effect profiles of four atypical antipsychotics

	Extrapyramidal side effects	Hyperpro-lactinaemia	Sedation	Weight gain	Orthostatic hypotension	Anticholinergic side effects
Risperidone	+	++	+	+	++	0/+
Olanzapine	0/+	+	++	+++	+	+/++
Quetiapine	0/+	0/+	++	++	++	0/+
Clozapine	0	0	+++	+++	+++	+++

Because there are such a large number of antipsychotics to choose from, people need not expect to suffer from side effects that they find to be unacceptable. If you feel that you are suffering from such side effects then speak to your psychiatrist or CPN about it. Many antipsychotic side effects can be controlled through diet and lifestyle changes, or by other medications that can be prescribed for you. Alternatively, the dose of the antipsychotic can be reduced or the antipsychotic can be changed to a different one.

The side effects most commonly seen in four atypical antipsychotic medications are summarized in Table 16.

Aripiprazole

Aripiprazole is a novel, so-called third-generation antipsychotic that has been described as a 'dopamine-serotonin system stabiliser'. It is purported to have good efficacy in treating positive symptoms, negative symptoms and mood symptoms and to be better tolerated than other antipsychotics. Principal side effects include headache, anxiety, insomnia, nausea, vomiting and light-headedness but *not* extrapyramidal side effects, hyperprolactinaemia, sedation or weight gain. As our understanding of schizophrenia improves, novel treatments such as aripiprazole are likely to continue emerging.

Antipsychotics in pregnancy and breast-feeding

Pregnancy

There is some scientific data to suggest that exposure to anti-psychotic medication during the first trimester of pregnancy is linked to a small additional risk of congenital abnormalities in the foetus. However, withholding antipsychotic medication may result in behavioural disturbances that expose the mother and foetus to much higher levels of overall risk. For this reason, pregnant women are generally advised to remain on antipsychotic medication for the full duration of their pregnancy.

Breast-feeding

Antipsychotic medications are excreted into breast milk, but except in the case of clozapine, breast-fed infants do not seem to suffer from this. Thus, a mother may decide to breast-feed whilst remaining on antipsychotic medication.

Starting antipsychotic medication

The starting dose of an antipsychotic is usually small so as to minimize any potential side effects. The dose is then increased according to the person's response, up to the minimum dose that is effective for that person. (This dose varies according to a large number of factors, including age, sex and weight.)

What if the chosen antipsychotic medication is ineffective?

If a person does not respond to the chosen atypical antipsychotic after a trial period of 6–8 weeks, the antipsychotic can be stopped and a different one started. If a person does not respond to two or more antipsychotics, an atypical antipsychotic called clozapine can be considered. Although clozapine is the most effective antipsychotic available, it requires registration with a monitoring service and, in the initial period, daily monitoring of vital signs as well as weekly blood tests. The blood tests monitor the white blood cell count, which can drop dangerously in up to 1 per cent of people on clozapine. The role of white blood cells is to fight off infections, so a drop in the white cell count can suddenly leave the body exposed to danger.

For how long should antipsychotic medication be taken?

Antipsychotics not only combat the symptoms of schizophrenia but also prevent the symptoms from recurring. If you have improved on a particular antipsychotic, you should continue taking it at the same dose for *at least* the next 6 months, preferably for the next 12–24 months and possibly for much longer.

What if taking antipsychotic medication is difficult?

Some people may be reluctant or unable to take their medication because, owing to the nature of their illness, they do not realize or accept that they are ill. Other reasons for not taking medication include side effects, delusional beliefs about the medication (e.g. that it is poison), fears of becoming addicted to the medication, poor concentration or motivation and a poor relationship with the doctor or key worker.

Missing tablets can lead to a relapse or recurrence of symptoms, as a result of which the schizophrenia sufferer may never regain his or her previous level of functioning. After a first psychotic episode, three-quarters of people who stop taking their medication suffer from a relapse within 1 year, compared to less than half of those who continue to take their medication.

For this reason it is particularly important for both you and your family to discuss any difficulties in taking your medication and to have these difficulties addressed. For example, your psychiatrist may be able to reduce the dose of your antipsychotic, change your antipsychotic to a different one or simplify your medication schedule.

'Depot' antipsychotics

Some people who have difficulties taking their antipsychotic medication may benefit from receiving it in the form of an injectable long-term preparation, or 'depot', instead of the usual oral tablet or oral liquid form. The principal advantages and disadvantages of depot versus oral antipsychotic medication are listed in Table 17. Before starting a person on a depot, it is usual to first administer an oral test dose. After about 7 days, the first depot dose is administered, and the dose is then increased at regular intervals as the oral antipsychotic is decreased and stopped. Depot injections are usually given every 7 or 14 days.

The commonly used typical, atypical and depot antipsychotics are listed in Table 18.

Table 17 Principal advantages and disadvantages of oral versus depot antipsychotics

	Advantages	*Disadvantages*
Oral medication	Short duration of action Flexible	Variable absorption from the gut Potential for poor compliance Potential for misuse and overdose
Depot medication	Less potential for poor compliance Less potential for abuse and overdose Regular contact with community psychiatric nurse or practice nurse, who gives the injection	Needle injections Potential delayed side effects Potential prolonged side effects Potential damage to relationship between the schizophrenia sufferer and his or her carers

Table 18 Commonly used atypical, typical and depot antipsychotics

Antipsychotic	Trade name	Licensed daily dose range in adults under the age of 65 years
Atypical antipsychotics (introduced from 1990)		
Risperidone	Risperdal	2–16mg (rarely exceed 10mg)
Olanzapine	Zyprexa	5–20mg
Quetiapine	Seroquel	50–750mg (usual dose range 300–450mg)
Amisulpiride	Solian	400mg–1200mg
Clozapine	Clozaril/Denzapine	25–900mg (usual dose range 200–450mg)
Aripiprazole	Abilify	10–30mg
Typical antipsychotics (introduced from the 1950s)		
Chlorpromazine	Largactil	75–1000mg
Fluphenazine	Modecate/Moditen	2–20mg
Haloperidol	Haldol/Dozic/Serenace	3–30mg
Pimozide	Orap	2–20mg
Flupenthixol	Depixol	3–18mg
Zuclopenthixol	Clopixol	20–150mg
Sulpiride	Dolmatil/Sulpitil/Sulpor	400–2400mg
Depot antipsychotics		
Risperidone	Risperdal Consta	Maximum: 50mg every 2 weeks
Fluphenazine decanoate	Modecate	Test dose: 12.5mg; maximum: 100mg every 2 weeks
Flupenthixol decanoate	Depixol	Test dose: 20mg; maximum: 400mg/week
Zuclopenthixol decanoate	Clopixol	Test dose: 100mg; maximum: 600mg/week
Pipiotazine palmitate	Piportil depot	Test dose: 25mg; maximum: 200mg every 4 weeks

Other drugs

A minority of schizophrenia sufferers may not respond to a seemingly adequate trial of antipsychotic medication. This is often because there are ongoing stressors in his or her life, because he or she is not taking the antipsychotic medication as prescribed or because he or she is using substances such as cannabis or cocaine. If such factors have been excluded or addressed and the schizophrenia sufferer continues not to respond to his or her antipsychotic medication, another anti-psychotic (usually from a different class or group) should be tried. Sometimes, other medications such as a benzodiazepine, lithium, or carbamazepine may be prescribed alongside an antipsychotic to 'augment' its effect: such augmentative strategies are usually *not* as effective as the antipsychotic clozapine and are therefore not generally used unless an adequate trial of clozapine has failed.

Keeping a treatment diary

You may find it helpful to keep a treatment diary in which you record the names of the different medications that you have been on, their benefits and their side effects. Such a treatment diary can help you and your doctor choose the best medication for you and can give you greater control over your illness. Table 19 shows an example of a treatment diary.

Table 19 My treatment diary

Medication	Dates taken	How taken	Positive effects	Side effects
Risperidone	15 January 2007 to 30 March 2007	Tablets Once a day before bed time	Voices almost disappeared Felt more relaxed Easy to take	Felt tired all day long Felt dizzy on standing up
Olanzapine	30 March 2007 to present	Tablets Once a day before bed time	Voices fully controlled Feel even more relaxed than on risperidone Easy to take	Initially put on 3kg (I have since lost this weight through diet and exercise)

8

Psychosocial treatments

The care of a schizophrenia sufferer is usually planned at one or several Care Programme Approach meetings. These meetings are useful to establish the context of the illness, evaluate current personal circumstances and formulate a detailed care plan to ensure that medical, psychological and social needs are met. As well as ensuring that the schizophrenia sufferer is receiving antipsychotic medication and is regularly reviewed by a member of the mental health-care team, the care plan may in due course involve a number of psychosocial measures, possibly including patient and family education, family therapy, cognitive-behavioural therapy, illness self-management, self-help groups, and social and vocational skills training.

Although under-utilized, psychosocial measures such as these can, alongside antipsychotic medication, play an important role in reducing symptoms, preventing relapse and re-hospitalization, and helping you to take control over your illness and subsequently, your life.

Expressed emotion

You might recall from Chapter 2 that 'expressed emotion' refers to critical, hostile or emotionally over-involved and overbearing attitudes directed at the schizophrenia sufferer by his or her relatives. These attitudes may take the form of negative comments or actions, or both, and may originate in a misunderstanding that the schizophrenia sufferer is in control of his or her illness and is 'choosing' to be ill. Alternatively, over-involvement may result from an unjustified sense of guilt about the schizophrenia sufferer's illness, or a desire to remove the burden of the illness from the schizophrenia sufferer and carry it upon one's own shoulders. A number of studies have demonstrated that high expressed emotion from relatives (and sometimes from other carers) is an important risk factor for relapse in schizophrenia, even though it may to a large extent reflect legitimate feelings of distress and anxiety about a loved one's illness.

Living in an environment with high expressed emotion is associated with a fourfold increase in the rate of relapse. The pressure from close relatives can be too much for the schizophrenia sufferer to bear, making him or her feel guilty, trapped and helpless, and pushing him or her back into an acute psychotic episode. Expressed emotion is sometimes measured through a taped family interview known as the Camberwell Family Interview, or simply by interviewing the schizophrenia sufferer. Families with high expressed emotion may be offered educational sessions, stress management, or family therapy: these can all help to reduce expressed emotion and can be important and integral parts of the joint care plan. If relatives have a good understanding of the nature of schizophrenia, they are likely to be more understanding of the needs and demands of the schizophrenia sufferer and therefore less likely to exhibit high expressed emotion.

Although family therapy requires a considerable investment of time and effort, it may be particularly helpful if there are fundamental difficulties in the way that family members relate to one another.

Once again, it cannot be stressed enough that families should not blame themselves for their relative's illness. Instead, they could be their relative's most valuable source of structure and support, and his or her greatest hope for a permanent recovery.

Cognitive-behavioural therapy

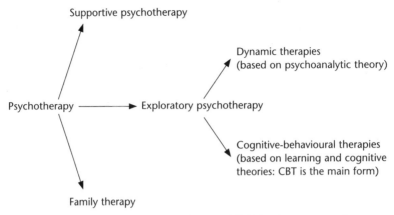

Figure 15 Cognitive-behavioural therapy (CBT) in the context of psychotherapy as a whole. The three main forms of psychotherapy, supportive psychotherapy, exploratory psychotherapy (in the form of CBT), and family therapy can all have a role to play in the management of schizophrenia. On balance, dynamic therapies based on psychoanalytic theory have not been proven effective in the management of schizophrenia.

Developed by Aaron Beck in the 1960s, cognitive-behavioural therapy is an increasingly common form of treatment for many psychiatric disorders. Although it is generally unsuitable during an initial episode of psychosis or during an acute psychotic relapse, it has been demonstrated to have long-term benefits on both positive and negative symptoms and to reduce the likelihood of re-hospitalization. It can also help to combat depression and increase functional and social skills. It is most often carried out on a one-to-one basis, but it can also sometimes be offered in small groups. In either case, it involves a limited number of sessions (typically between 10 and 20), each about 1 hour long. However, most of the work takes place outside the sessions (in the form of 'homework'). The schizophrenia sufferer and a trained therapist (who may be a psychologist, a counsellor, a doctor or a nurse) develop a shared understanding of the schizophrenia sufferer's current problems and try to understand them in terms of his or her thoughts, emotions and behaviour. This then leads to the identification of time-limited goals and of cognitive and behavioural strategies to achieve these goals. Thoughts are considered to be hypotheses that, through gentle questioning and guided discovery, can be examined, tested and modified. Behavioural tasks include self-monitoring, activity scheduling, graded task assignments and assertiveness training. In some cases, there may be an added focus on improving mood and self-esteem and on medication compliance and prevention of relapse.

Managing stress and anxiety

Stress and anxiety can make you more vulnerable to a relapse in your illness. You might recall that stress can result from life events such as losing a loved one, going through a divorce, losing your job or falling ill. But it can also result from seemingly smaller 'background' stressors such as constant deadlines, frustrations and conflicts. The cumulative effect of such background stressors can be far greater than that of any single life event. The amount of stress that a person can handle is largely related to his or her coping and thinking styles and level of social skills. People with positive coping and thinking styles and good social skills are better able to diffuse stressful situations; for example, by doing something about them, putting them in their correct context, or simply talking about them and 'sharing the pain'.

The first step in dealing with stress is to be able to recognize its warning signs. Study Table 20 and then write down on a piece of paper how you feel when you become stressed. Next make a list of situations in which you feel that way. For each situation on your list, think about one or more strategies that you can use to make it less stressful.

Table 20   Some of the symptoms of stress

Emotional symptoms	Anxiety, fear, irritability, anger, resentment, loss of confidence, depression
Psychological symptoms	Difficulty concentrating or making decisions, confusion, repetitive thoughts
Physical symptoms	Dry mouth, tremor, sweatiness, racing heartbeat, chest tightness and difficulty breathing, muscle tension, headache, dizziness
Behavioural symptoms	Nervous habits such as nail biting or pacing, drinking more coffee and alcohol, eating too much or too little, sleeping poorly, acting brashly or unreasonably, losing your temper, being inconsiderate of others, neglecting your responsibilities

Stressful situations	*Possible strategies for reducing stress*
Arguing with Liz	Talk to Liz about how I am feeling and try to resolve matters See her less often Avoid talking to her about certain things Walk away from an argument Use deep breathing
Receiving bills that I can't pay	Ask a relative to help me with my finances Speak to a social worker to see what help I can get Phone the bank and try to reach an agreement

Figure 16   Make a list of situations which you find stressful and for each situation think about one or more strategies for avoiding the situation or making it less stressful.

In Figure 16, certain problem-solving strategies are listed for reducing stress from the specific situations listed. However, there are also more general strategies that you can use for reducing stress. One common and effective strategy, called deep breathing, involves regulating your breathing:

- Breathe in through your nose and hold the air in for several seconds.
- Then purse your lips and gradually let the air out, making sure that you let out as much as you can.
- Continue doing this until you are feeling more relaxed.

A second strategy, often used in conjunction with deep breathing, involves relaxation exercises. Lying on your back, tighten the muscles in your toes for 10 seconds and then relax them completely. Do the same for your feet, ankles and calves, gradually moving up through your body until you reach your head and neck.

Other strategies that you can use for reducing stress include listening to classical music, taking a hot bath, reading a book or surfing the internet, calling up or meeting a friend, practising yoga or meditation, and playing sports.

Lifestyle changes can help to reduce stress as well as increase your ability to cope with stress. Lifestyle changes that you could consider include:

- Simplifying your life, even if this means doing less or doing only one thing at a time
- Having a schedule and sticking to it
- Getting enough sleep
- Exercising regularly; for example, walking, swimming, yoga
- Eating a balanced diet
- Avoiding excessive caffeine and alcohol
- Taking time out to do the things that you like doing
- Connecting with others and sharing your problems with them
- Changing your thinking style: having realistic expectations, reframing problems, expressing your feelings, maintaining a sense of humour

Such lifestyle changes are good not only for managing stress but also for your physical health and quality of life. Though individually small and simple, their cumulative effect can make a real difference to your chances of making a good recovery and avoiding a relapse.

If coping with stress continues to be a problem, consider asking a member of your mental health-care team whether you can be given relaxation training.

Coping with voices

Sometimes voices can in themselves be a significant source of stress and distress. Simple strategies to reduce or eliminate voices include:

- Keep a diary of the voices to help you to identify and avoid situations in which they arise
- Find a trusted person to talk to about the voices
- Focus your attention on an activity such as reading, gardening, singing or listening to your favourite music
- Talk back to the voices: challenge them and ask them to go away. If you are out in public, you can avoid attracting attention by talking into a mobile phone
- Manage your anxiety and stress using the techniques covered in this section
- Take your antipsychotic medication as prescribed
- Avoid drugs and alcohol

Staving off depression

Depression is common in schizophrenia, affecting as many as one in three schizophrenia sufferers. It can however sometimes be difficult to differentiate the symptoms of depression from negative symptoms or from the side effects of antipsychotic medication. The symptoms of depression are listed in Table 7, in Chapter 5. If you (or your relatives) suspect that you might be suffering from symptoms of depression, bring this to the attention of the mental health-care team. It is important to have a high index of suspicion, and to seek advice sooner rather than later. Thanks to antidepressant medication and talking treatments, depression is often successfully treated.

Antidepressant medication

Antidepressants are commonly used in the treatment of depression. Antidepressants may not be a solution to life's problems, but they may improve your mood and make it easier for you to address these problems. Modern antidepressants such as the serotonin-selective reuptake inhibitors (SSRIs) improve mood by increasing the amount of the chemical messenger serotonin in the brain. Examples of SSRIs are citalopram (Cipramil), sertraline (Lustral), fluoxetine (Prozac) and paroxetine (Seroxat).

Up to 70 per cent of people with depression respond to SSRIs, but improvement in mood may be delayed for 10–20 days so it is important to keep on taking the tablets. Better sleep is often the earliest sign of improvement.

SSRIs, like all medication, can have side effects, but they are generally safer and more tolerable than those of the older types of antidepressants. Common side effects include nausea, headache, dizziness, restlessness and sedation. These side effects, should they occur, tend to be mild and to disappear after the first few weeks of treatment. Some people may experience sexual dysfunction. This side effect doesn't usually disappear after the first few weeks of treatment so, if it is troublesome, the SSRI may need to be stopped and another antidepressant started. After recovering from depression, it is important to continue taking the antidepressant at the same dose for at least another 6–9 months, after which it can gradually be stopped. A common fear is that SSRIs are addictive. Although they result in flu-like symptoms if they are stopped suddenly after a long period of treatment, they are not addictive. In some cases an SSRI may fail to improve your mood significantly, in which case you may be changed to a different SSRI or to a different type of antidepressant.

Psychological treatments for depression

Although antidepressants are often the most readily available treatment option, psychological or talking treatments can in many cases be just as effective. They are often preferred by schizophrenia sufferers because they are (correctly) seen to address underlying problems rather than simply treating symptoms. Types of talking treatments that are especially appropriate for depression in schizophrenia are listed in Table 21. The type of talking treatment that is chosen depends on the schizophrenia sufferer's personal circumstances and preferences, but often also on the resources that are available in his or her local area. Although there is no substantial evidence for a marked benefit from combining a talking treatment with antidepressant treatment, this can certainly be considered in cases that are not responding to either.

Table 21   Psychological or talking treatments that can be used for depression in schizophrenia

Psychological treatment	What it involves
Counselling	Identification and resolution of current life difficulties Explanation, reassurance, and support
Cognitive-behavioural therapy	Identification of thinking errors and associated behaviours that occur in depression Correction of these thinking errors and behaviours
Interpersonal psychotherapy	A systematic and standardized treatment approach to personal relationships and life problems that may be contributing to depression
Family therapy	Identification and resolution of negative aspects of family relationships that may be contributing to depression

Common thinking errors in depression

Some of the common thinking errors (or 'cogitive distortions') in depression include:

- Arbitrary inference, i.e. drawing a conclusion in the absence of evidence. An example would be: 'The whole world hates me.'
- Over-generalization, i.e. drawing a conclusion on the basis of very limited evidence. An example would be: 'The shop-keeper gave me an angry look. The whole world hates me.'
- Magnification or minimization, i.e. over- or under-estimating the importance of an event. An example would be: 'The death of my cat means that I no longer have any reason to live.'
- Selective abstraction, i.e. focusing on a single negative event or condition while ignoring other more positive ones. An example would be: 'I'm not in a relationship' – even though I have a supportive family and am good at making friends.
- Dichotomous thinking, i.e. 'all-or-nothing' thinking. An example would be: 'If she doesn't come to see me today then she doesn't love me' – even though she's thinking about me all the time but has no transportation.
- Personalization, i.e. relating independent events to yourself. An example would be: 'The nurse left her job because she was fed up with me' – although she actually left for family reasons.
- Catastrophic thinking, i.e. expecting disaster to strike at any minute. An example would be: 'If I go out to the shops this afternoon I am more than likely to get run over.'

Things you can do to stave off depression

There are a number of things that you can do to stave off depression:

- Ask your doctor for help, and try to stick to any medication that he or she may prescribe.

- Break large tasks into smaller ones, set yourself realistic goals for completing them, and don't take on more than you can manage.
- Don't take any important decisions such as changing jobs or getting divorced while you are depressed. Thinking errors (see above) can lead you to make the wrong decision.
- Spend time with other people and talk to them about how you are feeling. You can also phone a helpline such as SANEline for practical advice and support.
- Let your family and friends help you. They may well be able to offer you the company, patience, affection, understanding, encouragement and support that you need.
- Get out of the house, even if this is just to buy a pint of milk or take a walk in the park.
- Do more of the things that you usually enjoy doing: read a book, go to the shops or cinema, visit friends – anything that takes your mind off your negative thoughts is likely to make you feel better.
- Take mild exercise.
- Get sufficient amounts of sleep. Even a single good night's sleep can make you feel much better.
- Use the techniques discussed in the previous section to reduce stress and anxiety.
- Fight your negative thoughts – perhaps the most important thing of all. Make a list of all the positive things about yourself (you may need to get help with this), keep it with you and read it to yourself several times a day. However bad you may be feeling, remember that you will not always be feeling this way. Have realistic expectations for yourself: improvements in mood are likely to be gradual rather than immediate, and there are going to be both good days and bad days.

Agree whom to call if you feel overwhelmed by suicidal thoughts. This may be a relative or friend, a helpline or your Community Mental Health Team. Carry the telephone numbers on you.

Staying off alcohol and drugs

Scientific research suggests that people who smoke cannabis are up to six times more likely to develop schizophrenia, and that people with schizophrenia who smoke cannabis have more frequent and more severe relapses of the illness. Other drugs that have been suggested to cause schizophrenia include stimulant drugs such as amphetamines, ecstasy and cocaine.

Once they are ill, many schizophrenia sufferers turn to alcohol or illicit drugs such as cannabis, amphetamines or cocaine to obtain relief from their symptoms or from their feelings of anxiety or depression. Alcohol and drugs may temporarily blunt or mask symptoms, but in the long term they are likely to lead to more frequent and severe relapses of the illness and to more severe anxiety and depression. You create a 'vicious cycle' in which the more you use alcohol and drugs to mask your symptoms, the worse your symptoms become, and the worse your symptoms become, the more you use alcohol and drugs. Alcohol and drugs may also delay you from getting help, including getting a prescription for antipsychotic medication.

Consequences of alcohol or drug use in schizophrenia sufferers

Possible consequences of using alcohol or drugs include:

- Increased psychotic symptoms
- Reduced treatment compliance and response
- Increased risk of relapse and re-hospitalization
- Increased risk of depression and anxiety
- Medical complications such as high blood pressure, heart attack, stroke, stomach ulcers or liver disease
- Complications of intravenous drug use such as hepatitis, HIV infection or venous thrombosis
- Family and marital difficulties

- Employment difficulties
- Motoring offences
- Accidents
- Financial hardship
- Criminal activity and its consequences

Simple advice and support is usually readily available from your Community Mental Health Team (CMHT). You may find it useful to ask a health-care professional to help you devise a goal-oriented management plan tailored to your needs. Tasks in this management plan could in the first instance include, for example, keeping your appointments, keeping a diary of substance use and taking your medication. Relatives can play an important role in supporting and monitoring progress and they should, if possible, be included in the management plan. They should try to adopt an open and non-judgmental approach, in an attempt to bolster their loved one's self-esteem and make him or her feel in greater control of the problem.

Alcohol or drug use is often prompted by stressful situations, so learning techniques for managing stress and anxiety, such as deep breathing and progressive muscle relaxation, can be particularly helpful (see pages 75–6), as is learning and role-playing specific social skills, which can then be used in stressful and high risk situations. Such social skills might include saying 'no' to a drug dealer or going into a pub and ordering a non-alcoholic drink.

If you find yourself in a stressful situation and are about to give in to temptation, don't! Call a relative or carer, talk through the situation, and get the support and encouragement that you need to pull through. Some schizophrenia sufferers also find support and encouragement in local support groups, or in more structured 12-step programmes such as Alcoholics Anonymous or Narcotics Anonymous. Ask your psychiatrist or key worker if such groups are suitable for you.

Alcoholics Anonymous

Founded in 1935 in Ohio, Alcoholics Anonymous is a spiritually oriented community of alcoholics whose aim is to stay sober and, through shared experience and understanding, to help other alcoholics to do the same, 'one day at a time', by avoiding that first drink. The essence of the programme involves a 'spiritual awakening' that is achieved by 'working the steps', usually with the guidance of a more experienced member or 'sponsor'. Members initially attend daily meetings in which they share their experiences of alcoholism and recovery and engage in prayer or meditation. A prayer that is usually recited at every meeting is the Serenity Prayer, the short version of which goes:

> God grant me the serenity to accept the things I cannot change,
> Courage to change the things I can,
> And the wisdom to know the difference.

Taking care of your physical health

Schizophrenia can encourage a number of unhealthy habits, and it can also make it difficult for you to start addressing these habits. Taking care of your physical health, however, not only increases life expectancy and quality of life but also promotes recovery and staves off anxiety and depression. You create a 'virtuous circle' in which the better you feel, the better you are able to take care of your physical health, and the better you are able to take care of your physical health, the better you feel.

Compared with other groups of people, schizophrenia sufferers are more likely to eat poorly, lack exercise and smoke. They are thus more likely to suffer from obesity, diabetes, cardiovascular problems such as high blood pressure, heart attack and stroke, and respiratory problems such as chronic bronchitis and emphysema. Some of the possible side effects of antipsychotic medication can directly or indirectly contribute to problems such as obesity and diabetes, making the care of your physical health all the more important.

Reasons for poor physical health in schizophrenia sufferers

Some of the common reasons for poor physical health in schizophrenia sufferers are:

- Poor diet
- Lack of exercise
- Smoking
- Alcohol and drug use
- Side effects of antipsychotic medication
- Social factors such as poor income and housing
- Poor monitoring of physical health

Physical health problems do not affect all schizophrenia sufferers, but it is important that you should have your physical health monitored so that any eventual problems can be detected early. Your general practitioner is normally able to carry out a physical check once every year. This usually involves weighing you, taking your pulse rate and blood pressure, and carrying out a blood or urine test. A physical check is a good opportunity to discuss your symptoms and medication, and to obtain advice on issues such as diet, exercise and smoking.

Diet

There are two separate factors to consider about your diet:

- Whether you are eating the right amount to keep your weight in the desirable range for health
- Whether you are eating a healthy balanced diet

Consult the height–weight chart (see Fig. 17) to check if you are the right weight for your height.

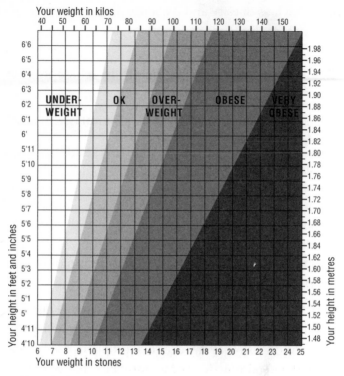

Figure 17   Height–weight chart

If you are underweight for your height this may be a cause for concern, and you should try to put on weight through eating sufficient quantities of a healthy balanced diet. If this fails or if you are significantly underweight, you should consult your general practitioner for advice.

If you are overweight for your height, try to cut down on the amount you are eating, especially on foods that are high in sugar or saturated and hydrogenated fats, and try to do more exercise. If you are fat or very fat for your height, you are at a high risk of physical health problems such as diabetes, high blood pressure, heart problems and stroke. It is particularly important that you try to lose weight, but be realistic about on most nights and causes distress or daytime effects such as fatigue, poor concentration, poor memory and irritability. These symptoms may not only delay your recovery but also predispose you to accidents, to psychiatric disorders such as anxiety and depression, and to medical disorders such as high blood pressure, infections, obesity and diabetes. Insomnia can also be caused or aggravated by poor sleep habits, depression, anxiety, stress, physical problems such as pain or breathing problems, medication, and alcohol and drug use (see Table 23). Short-term insomnia specifically is often caused by a stressful life event, a poor sleep environment or an irregular routine.

If you are suffering from insomnia, there are a number of simple measures that you can take to resolve or at least lessen the problem (see opposite).

Table 23 Some of the commoner causes of insomnia

Poor sleep habits
Psychiatric disorders
   Depressive disorder
   Mania and bipolar affective disorder
   Anxiety disorders
   Schizophrenia
   Post-traumatic stress disorder
   Chronic fatigue syndrome
Medical disorders
   Restless leg syndrome (thrashing about during sleep)
   Sleep apnoea (snoring with pauses in breathing during sleep)
   Chronic pain
   Chronic obstructive pulmonary disease
   Chronic renal failure
   Neurological disorders such as Parkinson's disease and other movement
      disorders
   Headaches
   Fibromyalgia
Other
   Alcohol and drug misuse
   Side effects of medication such as antipsychotic or antidepressant
      medication
   Shift working
   Caring for young children

what you can achieve: rather than go on to a 'crash diet' that is bound to end in failure, aim to lose small amounts of weight steadily over a long period of time. Cut back on foods that are high in sugar or saturated and hydrogenated fats such as fried foods, meat products, hard cheese, cream and butter. Eat three meals a day, but avoid snacking in between meals, especially on 'comfort' foods such as chocolate, cakes, biscuits and crisps. If you do feel like snacking, prefer a piece of fruit such as an apple, pear or banana. If you have had problems trying to lose weight in the past, consult your general practitioner or a dietitian for further advice.

If your weight is OK for your height, then you are eating about the right amount to keep your weight in the desirable range for health. This does not, however, mean that you are necessarily eating a healthy balanced diet.

A healthy balanced diet:

- Is based on starchy foods such as wholegrain bread, potatoes, pasta and rice
- Contains a lot of fruit and vegetables (five portions a day)
- Contains some protein-rich foods such as fish, poultry, meat, eggs and pulses
- Is low in fat, sugar, and salt

Tips for eating well

Here are eight tips for eating well from eatwell, the UK Food Standards Agency consumer advice and information website (<www.eatwell.gov.uk>):

1 Base your meals on starchy foods
2 Eat lots of fruit and vegetables
3 Eat more fish
4 Cut down on saturated fat and sugar
5 Try to eat less salt – no more than 6g a day
6 Get active and try to be a healthy weight

7 Drink plenty of water

8 Don't skip breakfast

If you are eating a healthy balanced diet you are probably getting all the vitamins and minerals that your body needs, and you do not need to take any dietary supplements.

Omega-3 fatty acids

Omega-3 fatty acids, found naturally in foods such as oily fish, linseed and eggs, have important functions in brain cells. A number of recent studies have suggested that omega-3 fatty acids may have benefits in schizophrenia if used as an adjunct to antipsychotic medication, but larger-scale research is needed to confirm these findings. On the other hand, there is little evidence that schizophrenia can be relieved through gluten-free or other special diets. If you intend to embark on a special diet or take dietary supplements, you should first consult your general practitioner or psychiatrist for advice.

Exercise

Regular exercise is an important part of looking after both your physical and mental health. With regard to physical health, exercise helps you to lose weight and maintain your target weight once you have achieved it. It also decreases your blood pressure and increases your physical strength, endurance and flexibility. Exercise usually improves the quality of your sleep, but it should not be taken just before bed time because its short-term alerting effects may prevent you from falling asleep (see page 89).

With regard to mental health, exercise helps to decrease stress, improve thinking and motivation, boost self-esteem and lift mood by causing the body to release increased amounts of chemical messengers called endorphins. Exercise also distracts you from positive symptoms such as hallucinations and

Table 22   Some of the benefits of exercise in schizophrenia

Weight loss
Improved physical strength, endurance and flexibility
Decreased stress
Decreased blood pressure
Better sleep
Improved thinking
Improved motivation
Better mood
Better self-esteem
Distraction from positive symptoms
Removal from emotional conflict
Increased social interactions

delusions, and some studies looking at exercise in schizophr have reported beneficial effects on these symptoms.

Exercise does not have to be difficult or intensive, an minutes of moderate activity a day is all that is neede improve your fitness. You could do some gardening, walk t shops, cycle, exercise at a gym or swimming pool, or play a sport such as basketball or football. In fact, there are so possibilities to choose from that you are bound to find that you enjoy doing. By getting you out of the house an of yourself', exercise can remove you from emotional co distract you from your symptoms, and increase the numb frequency of your social interactions. This in itself can beneficial effect on your mental health.

The particular benefits of exercise in people with phrenia are summarized in Table 22.

Sleep

Insomnia – difficulty in falling asleep or staying asleep – 30 per cent of the general population, but it is eve common in schizophrenia sufferers, in whom it can be effect of the illness. Insomnia is usually a problem if i

- Have a strict routine involving regular and adequate sleeping times (most adults need about 7–8 hours of sleep every night). Allocate a time for sleeping, for example, 11.00 p.m. to 7.00 a.m., and do not use this time for any other activities. Avoid daytime naps, or make them short and regular. If you have a bad night, avoid 'sleeping in' because this makes it more difficult to fall asleep the following night.

- Have a relaxing bedtime routine that enables you to relax and 'wind down' before bedtime. This may involve doing breathing exercises or meditation (see pages 75–6) or simply reading a book, listening to music or watching TV. Many people find it helpful to have a hot drink: if this is the case for you, prefer a herbal or malted or chocolaty drink to stimulant drinks such as tea or coffee.

- Sleep in a familiar, dark and quiet room that is adequately ventilated and neither too hot nor cold. Try to use this room for sleeping only, so that you come to associate it with sleep.

- If you can't sleep, don't become anxious and try to force yourself to sleep. The more anxious you become, the less likely you are to fall asleep, and this is only likely to make you more anxious! Instead, get up and do something relaxing and enjoyable for about half an hour, and then try again.

- Take regular exercise during the daytime, but do not exercise in the evening or just before bedtime because the short-term alerting effects of exercise may make it more difficult for you to fall asleep.

- Try to reduce your overall levels of stress by implementing some of the lifestyle changes detailed on page 76.

- Eat an adequate evening meal containing a good balance of complex carbohydrates and protein. Eating too much can make it difficult to fall asleep; eating too little can disturb your sleep and decrease its quality.

- Avoid caffeine, alcohol and tobacco, particularly in the evening. Also avoid stimulant drugs such as cocaine, amphetamines and ecstasy. Alcohol may make you fall asleep more easily, but it decreases the quality of your sleep.

If insomnia persists despite these measures, seek advice from your general practitioner or psychiatrist. In some cases, insomnia may have a clear and definite cause that needs to be addressed in itself – for example, a physical problem or a side effect of medication (see Table 23). Behavioural interventions such as sleep restriction therapy or cognitive-behavioural therapy can be helpful in some cases, and these therapies are generally preferable to sleeping tablets. Sleeping tablets can be effective in the short term but are best avoided in the longer term because of their side effects and their high potential for tolerance (needing progressively higher doses to achieve the same effect) and dependence. Sleeping remedies that are available without a prescription often contain an antihistamine that can leave you feeling drowsy the following morning. If you decide to use such remedies, it is important that you do not drive or operate heavy machinery the next day. Herbal alternatives are usually based on the herb valerian, a hardy perennial flowering plant with heads of sweetly scented pink or white flowers. If you are thinking about using a herbal remedy, speak to your general practitioner or psychiatrist first, particularly if you have a medical condition or allergy, are already on medication or are pregnant or breast-feeding.

Smoking

People with schizophrenia are nearly three times as likely to smoke as the average person, a higher rate than in any other mental illness. They are also more likely to smoke heavily, with dire consequences for their physical health, quality of life and life expectancy. Indeed, the most common causes of death in schizophrenia sufferers are cardiovascular and respiratory diseases that are themselves caused or aggravated by smoking.

Smoking also results in a decrease in blood levels of antipsychotic medication, such that smokers require higher doses of antipsychotic medication than non-smokers to achieve the same therapeutic effect. Assuming that a pack of 20 cigarettes costs an average of £5.23, someone smoking 40 cigarettes a day spends £3,817.90 on cigarettes each year. Though roll-up cigarettes are cheaper than filter cigarettes, they can also be more damaging to physical health.

Most schizophrenia sufferers who smoke started smoking before their illness began, suggesting either that smoking predisposes to schizophrenia or that the genetic or environmental factors that predispose to schizophrenia also predispose to nicotine addiction. An alternative explanation for the high rates of smoking in schizophrenia sufferers is that their illness makes them more likely to smoke, possibly because they feel that smoking enables them to relax or that it alleviates symptoms such as hallucinations and confusion.

A commonly held perception is that schizophrenia sufferers are unlikely to give up smoking and that it is unfair or even inhumane to try to deprive them of one of their principal pastimes and pleasures. The truth is that many schizophrenia sufferers are themselves highly motivated to stop smoking and are in need of all the help that they can get to fight what is often a severe nicotine addiction. Help can take the form of smoking cessation groups, behavioural therapy, nicotine replacement (e.g. in the form of patches or lozenges), and alternative therapies such as acupuncture and hypnosis. Success rates are highly variable from person to person, but it is important to keep persisting and not give up.

If you are motivated to stop smoking, mention this to your general practitioner or psychiatrist. Further information and support is also available from <www.netdoctor.co.uk/smoking/index.shtml>.

How to stop smoking

Make a list of the pros and cons of smoking. See Table 24 for an example of such a list.

Table 24   Pros and cons of smoking

Pros	Cons
Makes it easier to socialize with other smokers	Constant nagging from my partner
Makes me feel more confident in social situations	Bad breath putting my partner off
Provides me with momentary gratification	Constantly having to go outside, even in the cold and rain
Prevents cravings and withdrawal symptoms	The rancid smell in my house and on my clothes
	The effects on my health: sore throat, cough, shortness of breath, high blood pressure, stomach ulcers
	The effects on my appearance: looking 10 years older than I really am with yellow teeth, fingernails and skin
	Intense craving and withdrawal symptoms if I don't smoke
	Always needing a fix, and being unable to simply relax and enjoy life
	Feelings of inadequacy for not giving up
	Feelings of fear and anxiety at what I am doing to myself and how it will all end
	Feelings of guilt for the passive smoking endured by those around me
	The cost of it all, especially the fact that I can never afford a holiday

Keep your list with you and use it to motivate yourself to quit. Choose a date on which you want to quit and stick to it. Between now and that date keep a log of your smoking habits: record the times at which you 'light up', where you are, what you are doing and how you are feeling. Use this log to gain a better understanding of your smoking pattern. Once your chosen date arrives, make a clean break by throwing out all cigarettes and removing all ashtrays, lighters and matches. You are likely to experience intense cravings and withdrawal symptoms such as irritability, difficulty concentrating, tiredness, headache, increased appetite and insomnia. Nicotine replacement can help to relieve these cravings and withdrawal symptoms, so ask your general practitioner or psychiatrist to prescribe them for you. Cravings rarely last for more than a couple of minutes at a time, so diversion techniques such as chewing gum, brushing your teeth or doing a crossword may take your mind off them until they pass. If these diversion techniques fail, call a friend or relative who knows what you are going through and has agreed to give you help and support. Alternatively, read your list of pros and cons and use it to keep yourself motivated. Cravings are often triggered by certain places, activities and emotions that you have learned to associate with smoking. Use the log of your smoking habits to identify these places, activities and emotions, and try to think of alternative coping strategies.

Remember that cravings and withdrawal symptoms do not last for ever, and that in a matter of only days quitting will have become a much easier task! Don't be too harsh on yourself if you give in to temptation: put it behind you and keep on trying your best.

Coping with stigma

One of the most difficult challenges in recovering from schizophrenia is coping with the reactions of other people. Mental illness in general and schizophrenia in particular are heavily stigmatized by the general public. This is in large part due to ignorance and the fear that is born out of it, a fear that is sadly reinforced by the misrepresentation of schizophrenia sufferers in the media. Schizophrenia sufferers do not have split personalities, and as a group are neither unpredictable nor dangerous. They are not lazy or 'moral failures', and getting better is not simply a matter of them 'pulling themselves together'. Mental illnesses, like all medical conditions, have a biological basis and are not simply 'in the mind'.

It has been suggested that the genes that predispose to schizophrenia also confer an important adaptive advantage to mankind, namely, the ability for language and creativity. Some highly creative people have suffered from schizophrenia, including Syd Barrett, the early driving force behind the rock band Pink Floyd; John Nash, the father of 'game theory'; and Vaslav Nijinsky, the legendary choreographer and dancer. Similarly, many highly creative people have had close relatives affected by schizophrenia including the physicist Albert Einstein (his son), the philosopher Bertrand Russell (also his son), and the novelist James Joyce (his daughter).

Stigma can create a vicious cycle of alienation and discrimination that hinders progress to recovery by promoting social isolation, stress, depression, alcohol and drug misuse, unemployment, homelessness and institutionalization. Sadly, many schizophrenia sufferers report that stigma is just as distressing as the actual symptoms of their illness. In some cases schizophrenia sufferers fear stigma to such an extent that they find it difficult to accept that they are ill, and as a result do not seek out or accept the help that they need. For these reasons it is particularly important that carers analyse their attitudes and behaviours, and ensure that they are not involuntarily contributing to the stigma felt by the person that they are caring for. Attitudes and behaviours that contribute to stigma are often subtle, and may, for example, involve talking to the schizophrenia sufferer louder than is necessary, talking about him or her as if he or she cannot hear you, and failing to grant him or her sufficient independence and responsibility. A simple rule of thumb for carers is to behave towards the schizophrenia sufferer as they would to any other person: naturally, simply and with due respect and courtesy. Carers should try to be a 'refuge' or 'comfort zone' for the person that they are caring for, offering him or her practical and emotional support, but also the space and time to be quiet and alone. Deep questioning, argument and the venting of intense negative emotions are likely to overwhelm the schizophrenia sufferer and definitely need to be avoided.

Many schizophrenia sufferers feel unable to talk about their illness for fear of the pain and shame of being stigmatized. Being open about your illness may be a risk, but it also enables you to talk about your feelings and gain the support that you need. Learn as much as you can about your illness, so that you yourself can correct any false beliefs that people may hold about it. Try to educate friends and relatives about your illness and the issues surrounding it. If people use derogatory terms such as 'schizo' or 'psycho', remind them that their behaviour is unacceptable. If you feel that you are being unfairly treated as a customer or service user, make a complaint. You can even take a public stance against discrimination, for example, by speaking at events or writing about your experiences on a blog or in a local newspaper or magazine. Joining a local support group enables you to meet other schizophrenia sufferers and, at least temporarily, escape stigma. You can also use support groups to share your experiences and learn from and support one another.

Preventing relapses

Relapses in illness can have devastating consequences for the schizophrenia sufferer and his or her relatives and friends. After each relapse it becomes increasingly difficult to regain control over the symptoms, and this affects not only the schizophrenia sufferer's long-term outcome but also his or her quality of life. For these reasons, it is particularly important to try to prevent relapses.

There is strong scientific evidence that long-term anti-psychotic treatment substantially reduces rates of relapse and re-hospitalization in schizophrenia. If you are reluctant to take your antipsychotic medication because the schedule is too complicated or because you are suffering from side effects that you find unacceptable, then speak to your psychiatrist about this. Your psychiatrist may be able to simplify the schedule, decrease the dose or change you to an antipsychotic that suits you better. Do not simply stop taking your medication. Taking your medication at the dose prescribed by your psychiatrist is the single most important thing you can do to prevent a relapse in your illness. People with schizophrenia and their carers should learn to recognize the early signs and symptoms of a relapse. These signs and symptoms may differ from person to person, but common ones include:

- Suffering changes in mood
- Losing one's sense of humour
- Becoming tense, irritable or agitated
- Finding it difficult to concentrate
- Retreating from social situations and neglecting outside activities and social relationships
- Saying or doing irrational or inappropriate things
- Developing strange or unbelievable ideas
- Neglecting one's personal care
- Neglecting to take one's medication
- Dressing in unusual clothes or unusual combinations of clothes
- Sleeping excessively or hardly at all
- Eating excessively or hardly at all
- Becoming increasingly suspicious or hostile
- Becoming especially sensitive to noise or light
- Hearing voices or seeing things that other people cannot hear or see

If any of these signs and symptoms should arise, contact your local mental health-care team as soon as possible for support and advice, because this may help in averting a full-scale relapse. It is a good idea to have an action plan in place before problems arise and to have discussed this plan with your local mental health-care team. You can also keep a diary to help you identify the signs and symptoms of a relapse, should they arise. Remember that a relapse may impair your thinking and prevent you from recognizing those signs and symptoms. You may therefore need to rely on family and friends, and trust in their judgement.

Try to identify any factors that may have caused or contributed to your difficulties, because addressing these factors may help you to avert a full-scale relapse. Some of the most important of these factors are listed in Table 25 and discussed more fully in other sections of this book. Minimizing them can help you to prevent relapses and significantly improve your chances of a durable recovery.

Table 25 Some of the most important factors that may cause or contribute to a schizophrenic relapse

Non-compliance with medication or decreased dose of medication (see pages 66–7)

Alcohol and drugs (see pages 82–4)

High expressed emotion (see pages 71–2)

Stress (see pages 74–5)

Depression and anxiety (see pages 77–81)

Stigma (see pages 95–7)

Lack of social relationships and support

Poor physical health (see pages 84–95)

Lack of sleep (see pages 89–92)

Poor understanding of schizophrenia in general, and of signs of symptoms of relapse in particular

Caring, and caring for carers

According to Carers UK, each year in the UK over two million people take up a caring role, so you are certainly not alone. A good carer can be a schizophrenia sufferer's most valuable source of structure and support, and their greatest hope for a permanent recovery. Though you may feel that caring for a loved one is more a duty than a job, it is important that you identify yourself as a carer in order to obtain the help and support that all people in a caring role are in need of and entitled to.

Try to learn as much as you can about schizophrenia and to have a good idea of how it might affect the person that you are caring for. For example, the person that you are caring for may not be spontaneous in his or her responses to your questions. This may feel like he or she is ignoring you, but it is in fact because his or her thoughts are confused or because he or she is being distracted by voices. Understanding the illness builds up your confidence as a carer and gives you a clearer sense of what you might be able to achieve. Remember that there is only so much you alone can do to help the person you are caring for: being realistic about how much you can achieve enables you to prevent conflict, manage stress and avoid burnout. Speak to your local mental health-care team for further information about schizophrenia and for specific advice about caring for your relative. Information and advice is also available from voluntary organizations such as the ones listed in Useful addresses.

Caring for a schizophrenia sufferer is likely to require a lot of patience: schizophrenia sufferers have good days and bad days and tend to make progress in small steps. A relapse in the illness is likely to sap your morale, but it is important that you are prepared for this. It is a good idea to have an action plan in place before problems arise, and to have discussed this plan with your local mental health-care team. If problems arise, contact the mental health-care team sooner rather than later, as doing so may prevent any problems from getting worse. Remember that your caring role has made you an important source of information and expertise: learn to rely on your previous experiences and to trust in your judgement. At the same time, try to involve the person you are caring for in making decisions about his or her care.

Sometimes a schizophrenia sufferer may fail to recognize that he or she is ill, and so refuse to engage with the mental health-care team. In particular, he or she may insist that delusions and hallucinations are real or may be too paranoid to trust in carers. If the schizophrenia sufferer is refusing to engage with the mental health-care team, carers can try breaking the prospect of treatment into smaller, more manageable steps, starting with an initial appointment. If possible, give the schizophrenia sufferer a degree of choice in booking the appointment, and propose that you or someone else comes along.

As progress is usually made in small steps, it is easy for carers to lose sight of the fact that progress is actually being made. Try to feel positive about the person that you are caring for and to gently encourage and facilitate his or her progress. One of the most important things you can do as a carer is to ensure that the person you are caring for takes his or her antipsychotic medication as prescribed. Be on the lookout for any potential side effects (see pages 61–4), and do not hesitate to report any side effects to your local mental health-care team. Try to establish and maintain a simple daily structure and routine involving regular meal and sleeping times for the person you are caring for. Encourage him or her to attend appointments with members of the mental health-care team and other services.

Avoid nagging, criticizing, telling off, shouting, arguing and other markers of expressed emotion. Do not lose sight of the fact that high expressed emotion is an important predictor of relapse in schizophrenia, and ensure that you are giving the person you are caring for sufficient time and space to get better (see page 72). This can be difficult to achieve, because it is often a carer's instinct to try to do as much as possible for the person being cared for, and many carers have unrealistic expectations about the progress that the schizophrenia sufferer ought to be making. If you feel that this is an issue for you and the person that you are caring for, speak to your local mental health-care team about it. Families with high expressed emotion can be offered educational sessions, stress management or family therapy: these can all help to reduce expressed emotion and can be important and integral parts of a schizophrenia sufferer's care plan.

Finally, do not neglect other family members. Brothers and sisters of schizophrenia sufferers, particularly if they are young, may feel that they are not getting their fair share of your attention and may become jealous and resentful.

Caring for carers

Look after your physical and mental health

Carers need to care for themselves if they are to care most effectively for a significant other. Many carers come under severe stress and as a result suffer from serious health problems such as heart disease or mental illness. It is important that you recognize this and take it seriously if you are not to become ill and unable to fulfil your carer role. Use some of the techniques for stress management listed on pages 74–7 to reduce your levels of stress, and arrange for an annual health check-up to be carried out by your general practitioner. Make sure that you look after yourself, that you plan and pursue activities that you enjoy, and that you take a break or holiday from caring if you feel that you need one.

Get the emotional support that you need

Remember that you are not alone as a carer: share your opinions and experiences with the mental health-care team looking after the person you are caring for, and ask them for help and advice. Conversely, your perspective on the person you are caring for is invaluable to the team, so try to attend and participate in the regularly held Care Programme Approach meetings. Identify someone that you can talk to on a more personal level – perhaps a close relative or friend – about your experiences as a carer. Many family members and friends may find it difficult to discuss your caring role, and tend to underestimate the effort that you are making as a carer. The onus is on you to broach the subject and enlist their help and support. Joining a local carers' support group enables you to feel that you are not alone in your carer role, and such a support group can provide a valuable opportunity to learn from the experiences of other carers. Joining a carers' support group can also help you to understand any negative emotions that you may be harbouring, such as guilt, shame and anger, and to prevent these emotions from affecting the person that you are caring for.

Avoid blaming yourself or others

Parents sometimes think that schizophrenia is caused by bad parenting, and fear that they may be to blame for their son or daughter's illness. Their feelings of guilt can come to dominate family life, and add to the heavy burden already carried by their son or daughter. In the 1940s some psychoanalysts believed that certain mental illnesses such as schizophrenia and autism resulted from having a so-called 'refrigerator mother', an emotionally absent and therefore inadequate mother. This theory and other similar theories have never found scientific backing, and have long since been discredited and discarded. In fact, scientific research increasingly indicates that schizophrenia is a biological illness of the brain.

Parents also sometimes look around for someone else to blame for their son or daughter's illness, such as the general practitioner, the psychiatrist, or even their son or daughter. That they should do so is natural and understandable since it helps them to make sense of the illness of a loved one. Nevertheless, it is important that they should remember that the real 'culprit' is ultimately a biological illness of the brain. They should avoid playing the 'blame game' and instead focus their energies on the challenging journey to recovery.

Like guilt and blame, frustration and anger can be a normal reaction to the illness of a loved one. Parents often have thoughts such as, 'Why did this happen to our family?' or even, 'Why should I even bother? It's too much hard work and, ultimately, it's all going to be for nothing.' Sometimes parents may direct their anger and frustration at their son or daughter, even though they realize that he or she is not to blame for the illness. Unchecked anger adds to your stress and to that of your son and daughter, and thereby prevents your family from moving ahead. Although you cannot change the reality of the illness, you can change your reaction to it. Try diffusing your anger by talking about the feelings that underlie it: talk to relatives, friends, mental health-care professionals and other families affected by schizophrenia. Or else try channelling your anger so that it becomes a force for good; for example, by motivating you to seek out help for your family.

Get the practical support that you need

You can obtain an assessment of your needs as a carer by asking your general practitioner to refer you to local Social Services or by referring yourself directly to them. A carer's needs assessment is often helpful in ensuring that your practical needs as a carer are met. You can find out about the carer support services available in your area through Social Services, through a local carers' organization, or through Carers UK and their dedicated phone line, CarersLine. Such services may include help at home, aids and equipment, break services and day care, among others. Many carers are reluctant to claim social benefits, either because they have never done so before or because they are put off by the complicated rules and difficult forms.

As a carer you play an important role in society, and the benefits that you are entitled to exist to recognize and support that role. Some of these benefits are detailed on pages 107–9, and you can obtain help in claiming them from your local mental health-care team, local Social Services or voluntary organizations such as Carers UK.

Your life outside your caring role

Being a carer is highly stressful and can become all-encompassing. It is important that you think about yourself and your future, as a time may come when you are no longer required to be a carer. As the condition of the person you are caring for improves, he or she may become more independent and in some cases may move out to an apartment or a group home. When this happens carers often find themselves lacking in purpose and direction, and unable to adjust to their changed circumstances. For this and other reasons it is vital that you continue to plan and pursue activities that you enjoy, and that you keep up your life outside of your caring role. Many carers are able to be employed in a part-time job, and this can be both a salutatory distraction from the stress of caring and an invaluable source of additional income. Similarly, some carers are able to further their skills, for example with evening courses or a part-time degree.

Siblings

As parents focus their attention on their ill son or daughter, they run the risk of becoming less available to their other children. These children are also in need of parental attention, as they are likely to have been profoundly affected by the illness of their brother or sister. They may be anxious for their family and fearful of developing the illness themselves. Schizophrenia often strikes in the prime of life, at a time when young people are launching into life – starting college or university, getting a first job or enjoying an expanding range of activities and relationships. For this reason, siblings may find it particularly difficult to enjoy their successes while witnessing their ill brother or sister slipping further and further behind. At the same time, they may feel pressured to achieve more so as to 'compensate' for their brother or sister's illness and not to add to the concerns of their afflicted parents.

Siblings should not blame themselves or anybody else for their brother or sister's illness or let it prevent them from enjoying their life outside of the family. By nurturing old friendships, they are able to obtain support and talk through difficult feelings such as anger, anxiety and guilt. Parents need to make a special effort to remember the needs of siblings, and to ensure as far as possible that they are included in family discussions surrounding the illness. Siblings should educate themselves as much as possible about schizophrenia, and also consider joining a carers' support group. Older siblings may be able to play an active role in caring and in due course become an invaluable source of support and respite to their parents.

If siblings feel that they are not getting the parental attention that they need, they should not feel afraid to ask for it.

Driving and schizophrenia

You should stop driving during a first psychotic episode or psychotic relapse of your illness, as this can seriously endanger lives. In the UK, you must notify the Driver and Vehicle Licensing Agency (DVLA). Failure to do so makes it illegal for you do drive and invalidates your insurance. The DVLA then sends you a medical questionnaire to fill in as well as a form asking for your permission to contact your psychiatrist. Your driving licence can generally be reinstated if your psychiatrist can confirm that:

- Your illness has been successfully treated with medication for a period of at least 3 months
- You are conscientious about taking your medication
- The side effects of your medication are not likely to impair your driving
- You are not misusing drugs

Further information on schizophrenia and driving can be obtained from the DVLA website at <www.DVLA.gov.uk>. Note that the rules for professional driving are different from those described above.

Social benefits

Every year in the UK millions of pounds of benefits are left unclaimed, often by people with a mental illness and their carers. Some of the benefits available to people with a mental illness and their carers are detailed here. For further information on these benefits, see the Department for Work and Pensions website, <www.dwp.gov.uk/lifeevent/benefits>, contact your local Citizens Advice Bureau, or get in touch with local Social Services.

Housing benefit and council tax benefit

Housing benefit and council tax benefit are means-tested, tax-free payments made to people who need help paying their rent and their council tax, respectively. Both benefits are administered by the local authority in whose area the property is situated. These benefits do not cover mortgage interest payments.

Income support

Income support is a means-tested payment made to people who are between the ages of 16 and 59 who work less than 16 hours a week and who have a reason for not actively seeking work (on grounds of disability, caring for children, or caring for relatives).

Claimants of Income Support are also entitled to other benefits such as housing benefit and council tax benefit (see above).

Social fund

Social fund payments are payments, grants or loans made in addition to certain benefits for important intermittent expenses that cannot be met by normal income.

Incapacity benefit

Incapacity benefit is paid to people who cannot work because of illness or disability and who cannot get statutory sick pay from their employer. It is related to national insurance contributions and requires regular medical certificates. It is not means-tested.

Disabled person's tax credit

The disabled person's tax credit is for people beyond the age of 16 who work an average of 16 hours a week or more and who have an illness or disability that restricts the amount that they can earn.

Disability living allowance

Disability living allowance is paid to people under the age of 65 who are in need of personal care or help with getting around, or both. It is not means-tested.

Attendance allowance

Attendance allowance is paid to people aged 65 or more who need help with personal care because of an illness or disability. It is not means-tested.

NHS costs

Depending on your circumstances you may qualify for free NHS prescriptions and hospital medicines, free NHS dental treatment and free NHS eyesight tests, and other NHS costs may be met too.

Carer's allowance

Carer's allowance is a means-tested, taxable weekly benefit payment made to people who look after someone who is receiving attendance allowance or disability living allowance at the middle or high rate of care. Among other stipulations, the carer must be over 16 years of age and spend 35 hours a week or more in his or her caring role. The carer does not have to be related to or living with the person he or she is caring for.

Useful addresses

General

Carers UK
20–25 Glasshouse Yard
London EC1A 4JT
Tel.: 020 7490 8818
CarersLine: 0808 808 7777 (free; provides information and advice on Wednesdays and Thursdays, 10 a.m. to 12 noon, 2 p.m. to 4 p.m.)
Website: www.carersuk.org

Carers give so much to society, yet as a consequence of caring they can experience ill health, poverty and discrimination. The organization's members seek to end this injustice by: mobilizing carers and supporters; campaigning for change; carrying out research; and transforming the public perception of what caring is about.

Crisis
66 Commercial Street
London E1 6LT
Tel.: 0870 011 3335
Website: www.crisis.org.uk

Provides help and support to homeless people or people in danger of becoming homeless, so that they can rebuild their lives and not remain trapped in the cycle of homelessness.

Depression Alliance
212 Spitfire Studios
63–71 Collier Street
London N1 9BE
Tel.: 0845 123 23 20
Website: www.depressionalliance.org/

The leading UK charity for people with depression, Depression Alliance provides services including publications, supporter services, local self-help groups and a pen-friend scheme. It also carries out research into depression, raises public awareness of the condition, and campaigns for changes to mental-health policy and practices.

Hyperguide to the Mental Health Act
Website: www.hyperguide.co.uk/mha/

This succinct guide to the Mental Health Act has been set up by Nigel Turner, a concerned individual, and is free to users, although some prohibitions apply.

Making Space
Website: www.makingspace.co.uk

Helps all those with schizophrenia and other forms of mental illness. The current area of operation includes Cheshire, Cumbria, Derbyshire, Greater Manchester, Lancashire, Merseyside, Staffordshire and Yorkshire. Services offered include family and carer support, befriending schemes, day centres, education and training schemes, residential care homes, supported housing schemes, and short breaks and holidays.

Mind (National Association for Mental Health)
15–19 Broadway
London E15 4BQ
Tel.: 020 8519 2122
MindinfoLine: 0845 766 0163 (9.15 a.m. to 5.15 p.m., Monday to Friday, local rate calls throughout UK)
Website: www.mind.org.uk

Advances the views, needs and ambitions of people with mental-health problems, and campaigns for their rights; challenges discrimination and raises public awareness of mental-health issues. Mind offers, through 200 local associations, supported housing, crisis helplines, drop-in centres, counselling, befriending, advocacy, employment and training schemes, and other support services. The information line offers confidential help and also a special legal service.

Rethink (formerly the National Schizophrenia Fellowship)
Head Office, Fifth Floor
Royal London House
22–25 Finsbury Square
London EC2A 1DX

Registered Office
28 Castle Street
Kingston-upon-Thames KT1 1SS
Tel.: 020 8974 6814 (national advice service: 10 a.m. to 3 p.m. Monday,
Wednesday, Friday; 10 a.m. to 1 p.m. Tuesday, Thursday)
Website: www.rethink.org

Rethink offers over 350 services and has more than 130 support groups
nationally. The range of services includes advocacy, carer support,
community support, employment and training, helplines, housing,
nursing and residential care, and services dedicated to black and minority-
ethnic communities. The organization also produces a quarterly magazine,
Your Voice, and a range of other publications.

Royal College of Psychiatrists
Website: www.rcpsych.ac.uk/mentalhealthinformation.aspx

This professional and educational organization for psychiatrists in the UK
and Republic of Ireland produces a range of high-quality materials for the
general public including various leaflets on schizophrenia, and treatments
such as CBT and depot medication. This particular site is an online
mental-health resource.

Samaritans
National Helpline: 08457 90 90 90 (24 hours a day, 365 days a year; local
rate)
Write to: Chris
PO Box 90 90
Stirling FK8 2SA
Website: www.samaritans.org.uk
Email: jo@samaritans.org

In their own words, Samaritans are 'always here to listen . . . with an
open mind for as long as you need'. They provide confidential non-
judgemental support for those experiencing feelings of distress and
despair, as well as for those who feel suicide is the only answer.

SANE (Schizophrenia A National Emergency)
First Floor, Cityside House
40 Adler Street
London E1 1EE
Tel.: 020 7375 1002
SANEline: 0845 767 8000 (local rate calls, 1 p.m. to 11 p.m. 365 days a year)
Website: www.sane.org.uk

Campaigns for better services and treatments for people with serious mental illness and undertakes research into its causes. SANEline provides confidential information, crisis care and emotional support for those experiencing mental-health problems, their families and carers; calls may be anonymous.

The Sleep Council
High Corn Mill
Chapel Hill
Skipton
North Yorkshire BD23 1NL
Tel.: 0845 058 4595 (admin)
Freephone leaflet line: 0800 018 2923
Website: www.sleepcouncil.com
Email: info@sleepcouncil.org.uk

Provides useful general advice on sleep and beds.

Help with alcohol- and drug-related problems, including smoking

Alcoholics Anonymous
Registered Office
PO Box 1
Toft Green
York YO1 7NJ
National helpline: 0845 769 7555 (24-hour; confidential)
Website: www.alcoholics-anonymous.org.uk

A spiritually oriented community of alcoholics whose aim is to stay sober and, through shared experience and understanding, to help other alcoholics to do the same, 'one day at a time', by avoiding that first drink. The essence of the programme involves a 'spiritual awakening' that is achieved by 'working the steps', usually with the guidance of a more experienced member or 'sponsor'.

Al-Anon
Website: www.al-anonuk.org.uk

Offers understanding and support for families and friends of problem drinkers. At the group meetings members receive comfort and understanding and learn to cope with their problems through the exchange of experience, strength and hope. Members learn that there are things they can do to help themselves and, indirectly, to help the problem drinker. Alateen is part of the Al-Anon fellowship and is for young people aged 12 to 17 who are affected by a problem drinker.

Cocaine Anonymous UK
PO Box 46920
London E2 9WF
Tel.: 0800 612 0225 (10 a.m. to 10 p.m., daily)
Website: www.cauk.org.uk

A fellowship of men and women who share their experience, strength and hope with one another so that they may solve their common problem and help others to recover from their addiction. The only requirement for membership is a desire to stop using cocaine and all other mind-altering substances.

Drinkline
Tel.: 0800 917 8282 (Freephone; 9 a.m. to 11 p.m., Monday to Friday)

The National Alcohol Helpline and a confidential service that offers information and support both to callers and to their relatives and friends.

QUIT
Quitline: 0800 00 22 00 (free)
Website: www.quit.org.uk
Email: stopsmoking@quit.org.uk (counselling)

This organization's mission statement is to provide practical help, advice and support to all smokers who want to stop.

Index